T0158873

ALSO BY VICTOR D'AMICO

Smart Presentations

Sharing a Lifetime Passion for Europe

Bonding with Piedmont

RECOLLECTIONS

Things Hard to Forget

VICTOR D'AMICO

iUniverse, Inc.
New York   Bloomington

Recollections
Things Hard to Forget

iUniverse books may be ordered through booksellers or by contacting:

iUniverse
1663 Liberty Drive
Bloomington, IN 47403
www.iuniverse.com
1-800-Authors (1-800-288-4677)

Because of the dynamic nature of the Internet, any Web addresses or links contained in this book may have changed since publication and may no longer be valid. The views expressed in this work are solely those of the author and do not necessarily reflect the views of the publisher, and the publisher hereby disclaims any responsibility for them.

ISBN: 978-1-4502-4573-9 (pbk)
ISBN: 978-1-4502-4575-3 (cloth)
ISBN: 978-1-4502-4574-6 (ebk)

Printed in the United States of America

iUniverse rev. date: 8/12/10

To my children and their children

Contents

Acknowledgments

I must thank my wife Yvonne for the help she gave me in writing this book. She shared so many of my recollections and assisted me in recalling them. Reliving these moments gave us both much pleasure. Her reading and offering suggestions, then editing and proofing my material made it a better manuscript.

Mike Mirolla, my mentor at Winghill Writing School, gave me suggestions, but mostly it was his complimentary remarks that encouraged me to put together my assignments into a book.

Sheila Lange's grammatical editing turned my manuscript into a document that read much more smoothly.

Introduction

This book is a collection of pieces written for an Internet course given by the Winghill Writing School located in Ottawa, Canada. After my retirement and before taking the course, I had written and self-published three books. The first one was titled *Smart Presentations*, which gave guidance to a person trying to prepare and give a presentation. It was based on my experiences working for General Electric and as a technical manager for a European consortium. Several years of business traveling in Europe and then working for four years in Munich, Germany, gave me the opportunity to visit many countries as both a tourist and a working professional. My wife and I described many of the adventures from these years in a book entitled *Sharing a Lifetime Passion for Europe*. During my time in Europe I made numerous visits to the town of Ivrea and the village of Vestigne located in the Piedmont province of Italy. It was the area where my wife Yvonne's parents grew up, and over the years I grew familiar with the people, the land, and its history. This attachment encouraged me to write a book entitled *Bonding with Piedmont*.

I never expected a large circulation for these books, but hearing from people who read them express their enjoyment at sharing my experiences gave me satisfaction and encouragement. A positive review of the last book on an Internet Web site gave a slight boost to my royalty payments.

During my career as a radar engineer and manager, I found that I received satisfaction from writing reports, making presentations, and producing proposals. Putting together technical material so it was easily understood and presented ideas in a positive way seemed to satisfy my creative need. After I retired, I was asked by the consortium I had worked for to generate a technical marketing brochure that would describe the features and characteristics of the system I had helped to develop for four years. With the aid of a professional graphics designer, I produced a document that was well received and piqued my interest in writing. The result was the three books referred to above.

In exploring ways to satisfy my attraction to writing, I discovered the Winghill Writing School, which offers several courses catering to different student interests. I selected a creative writing curriculum that presents a variety of forms in which to express yourself. However, I soon found out that my assignment submissions dealt mainly with my memoirs and family history. I seemed to lack the imagination to invent conflicts and produce fiction pieces. In my struggles to create ideas, I gained a great deal of appreciation for the inventiveness of the authors I read and the research effort they had undertaken to produce their material. I soon realized my writing ambitions were very modest in comparison.

I gravitated to writing on topics and events that were not only part of my traveling adventures, but those subjects that described recollections that left lasting impressions—for example, my somewhat different route through college and my experiences entering the army and teaching in college. However, I could not avoid my overseas exploits, so I tried to give the stories a little different slant. I also focused on family escapades like my children's weddings, my fiftieth wedding celebration, or cooking my wife's favorite dish.

The longest piece was my attempt to write a biography about my mother-in-law. She lived to be ninety-eight years old and spent part of her last thirty years living with my wife and me. In many ways she was a very distinct personality and left me with many things to remember about her.

In writing this book, the intent was to have each episode stand on its own as a separate complete subject. Therefore, there is some repetition of certain events or thoughts to achieve this objective.

The comments I received from the tutor to whom I submitted my assignments have been both helpful and encouraging; a writer appreciates positive feedback. It gave me confidence that others, especially my family, might enjoy my recollections.

Growing Up

*By recalling some of the events in my early years growing up
and comparing them with those occurrences in raising my own
children, I am able to highlight some differences in a generation.*

I was the oldest of three children, with a sister who was eighteen months younger and a brother who was born five years after I came along. My parents started their family in the year that the Great Depression began in 1929, and I am sure their early years of marriage must have been a struggle. They were both born in the United States of parents that came to this country in the late nineteenth century. Neither of them shared much of their past with either me or my siblings, so we knew little of their early life. They both had a limited formal education and found themselves in the working world at an early age. My mother, like many women, found employment in the garment factories, where she became quite skilled; this talent served her well later in life. She was hardworking, but somewhat sheltered and naïve in the ways of the world. My father was just the opposite, and his street smarts included an ability to promote himself. He started out trying to sell real estate, but during my childhood he spent most of his time selling wine to liquor stores. During the war he worked at a nearby war plant, where he became a union shop steward, but once the war ended he returned to his wine-marketing vocation.

My parents never had enough money to open a savings account even though my mother worked most of her life sewing clothes. She was very talented in this endeavor and could make a suit or dress for a woman after just being presented the fabric and being shown a picture of the garment. This work occupied much of her time, and although money was often scarce, she never neglected putting an appetizing dinner on the table each night. We children would often go our separate ways, but we always assembled each day for our main meal.

My father at all times had a job, was well liked, and was very suited to being a salesman. He didn't drink or frequent bars, but his weakness was the need to gamble; his favorite outlets were betting on bocce games, playing cards, or wagering on horse races. It was probably the reason he never had any money to put in the bank. He had a strong sense of family and was a strict disciplinarian. An occasional slap in the head would signal his disapproval. His family duties extended to housing my mother's sisters when they encountered personal marriage problems. Like most fathers of that time, he had very little involvement in the activities of his children.

Most family outings consisted of visits during the holidays to the homes of relatives, where ample food was shared and an occasional card game was played. A special occasion I remember occurred when my mother took my sister and me to the World's Fair when I was ten years old. After sightseeing all day, she even managed to find the money to take us to a spectacular nighttime water show starring Esther Williams, a very popular Hollywood celebrity. I never forgot the disappointment I felt because my father never found the time to take me to this wonderful exhibition that was located only ten minutes by train from our house.

I recall living in a rented two-bedroom apartment over a corner grocery store not far from a typical New York City playground. It was a place where you could play softball, basketball, or handball, chin on a high bar, ride the swings or seesaw, or go down a slide. It had something for everybody. Of course, if you took part in a softball game, you had to learn to avoid all the obstacles on the field. If you played right field, you had to position yourself on the narrow side of the handball wall to cover the field. In center field, you had to contend with basketball backboards; and in left field, you had to get around the monkey bars.

My early years were spent on the streets near my house playing stoopball or other simple games like punchball with neighborhood kids. The former game only required two people: one player would bounce a rubber ball off the steps of the stoop, hoping to get the ball beyond the reach of the defensive player. The number of ball bounces or the distance traveled would determine what success was achieved. It was like playing a two-man baseball game and helped develop good eye/hand coordination for later participation in team sports. When I got older, I advanced to another form of a baseball game, where a rectangle painted on a wall was a target strike zone and the player in front of it would try and hit your pitches with a bat. Three-man basketball games were also very popular and very competitive, because if you lost, your team watched for a while. It seemed as if there was always something to do, and there were never any adults needed to help organize activities.

Playing outside was always the preferred way of occupying my spare time, but I also managed to find things I could do by myself. I spent endless hours playing with an erector set I was given one Christmas, and I discovered a baseball game I could play with dice. I created a league of teams and kept track of the games played between them. I obviously didn't need any help to keep myself amused.

My parents never read me stories, but somehow the library near the grammar school attracted my attention and I enjoyed such books as *Bomba, the Jungle Boy*. However, I became involved with more modern and adult books when I was hired to work in a business whose time has now passed. Next door to where I got my haircuts was a small store rented by two men who ran a rental lending library business. One day, when I was in the eighth grade, they approached me and asked if I wanted a job. They bought recently published books and distributed them to candy stores and drugstores. At one time almost every block in New York City had a candy store where one bought ice cream, sundaes, sodas, cigarettes, newspapers, and—yes—candy. Many people visited these establishments each day, and the stores were an ideal site for a lending library, where for a small fee you could rent a book. New bestsellers would cost about twenty-five cents for several weeks, while older books might rent for as little as ten cents. They wanted me to reinforce the jackets of new book purchases with a heavy brown paper that had one side that became adhesive when wetted. It was important to preserve the flashy covers to attract a reader's attention. At other times I would repair the spines of older books, and during the summers I would help them deliver new books to their clients. I held this job through four years of high school, and it helped me pay for the train fare I needed to get to school, feed the cigarette smoking habit I acquired, go to a movie on a weekend, and take a girl on a date. I never had to ask my father for money; in fact, at times I gave him part of my wages. The advent of pocket books soon made this type of business uncompetitive, but I appreciated the opportunity it had given me.

After I entered high school, I left the streets of the nearby neighborhood to play with the bigger boys at the park or school yard, where teams were organized and games were more competitive. Softball occupied most of my time, and I played any position that needed to be filled. I remember one contest where I was pitching and the teams unknowingly selected my younger brother to umpire balls and strikes. I believe I won that game! We played in some organized leagues, but our most exciting games were when we bet money on our team to win. One time we played a very good team and paid a pitcher to perform for us so we could be more competitive. Winning that game caused a lot of celebration.

My father encouraged my playing softball by coming to many of the games, but he forbade me to play football. Of course, I didn't agree with his opinion, and my attempts to play were made complicated. I managed to borrow a helmet, shoulder pads, and pants and hid them in the hall closet. Keeping this activity secret was difficult, because when I came home from playing there was always some part of me that ached and hiding my discomfort was a real challenge. The struggle to cover up my playing started to dampen my enthusiasm for the sport. When I cut my tongue playing without a mouthpiece and my father found out about the deception, my football career came to an end.

I hung out with a group from high school, friends that played at the grammar-school yard and a much larger crowd at the city park that some called a gang. Although they were often mischievous, they were rather tame compared to present-day gangs. However, on the night that President Roosevelt died, we got into a bit of trouble. We were drinking beer in a small park that had a narrow entrance and benches that were surrounded by hedges. Someone who had too much to drink decided he wanted to get rid of his empty bottle by throwing it out into the busy street next to the park. It came down in front of a police car that was passing by, and before we knew it, two policemen had corralled ten of us. They took down our names, addresses, and ages, and they said our parents would soon be hearing from the police. None of us were smart enough to give phony information, and we nervously waited for the next stage of justice to unfold. Each day, starting with the oldest boy, a different parent was informed of our wrongdoing. To have all the culprits face the punishment of the parents was enough satisfaction for the authorities. I got lucky. Since I was younger than many of the boys, my parents never received any notification, but the anxiety I endured waiting served to teach me a lesson.

As I reflect back on these incidents from my growing up, I wonder what it told me about myself and the influence of my parents. They were typical of parents at that time. They saw their role as putting food on the table and clothes on your back and instilling in you a strong sense of discipline. The lack of direct adult involvement in what I did seemed to instill in me a strong sense of independence, and I did most things by myself or with a small group of friends. Except for sharing meals together and visiting relatives, I did little with my brother and sister. My sister, who was close to my age, attended a different high school, and when my brother started in high school, I was already in college; thus aside from contact within our house, we went our separate ways.

I routinely traveled throughout the city as I went about my days. In high school I rode the subway back and forth to Brooklyn from Queens each day for an hour. On weekends I would often go to Jamaica, about a half hour from home, to see a movie with a friend. During the summer, groups of us would hitchhike to Rockaway Beach to enjoy the ocean. On rare occasions, we journeyed across Manhattan to Newark to see a burlesque show. In college I took my father's car from Queens to pick up a date in Brooklyn, and then drove to a fraternity party in the Bronx. During my youth I never ventured beyond the environs of New York, but I considered a good part of the city my playing field.

My parents knew that I traveled around a lot, but they weren't overly concerned because most of the Big Apple at that time was relatively safe. I couldn't ask advice from my parents because I felt their growing up was so different from what I was going through, but that's probably what most children think about their parents. My mother was so proud of the meals she put on the table for us. You knew it was Thursday when pasta with tomato sauce was served. On Sundays meatballs were added to the sauce; and I remember, when I came home late on a Saturday night, making a sandwich of the browned meatballs was my favorite snack. It wasn't fancy, but it was Italian comfort food and there was usually plenty of it. My father didn't wait for you to ask for advice; he spoke his mind on a subject and his pronouncements were often expressions of control. My sister especially noticed his attempts to manage our lives.

Without any help from parents, I found out about and enrolled in a recently organized junior college with a work-study program. Wages from my working semesters allowed me to pay for the time I spent in classes. With the money I saved and some financial help from my parents, I was able to attend New York University and eventually received an engineering degree. My sister received no encouragement to enter college and started working after graduating from high school; she contributed to the family income. At that time higher education for women was not a high priority. My brother was more fortunate, since his athletic ability earned him a full scholarship to St. John's University.

My family never had much, but I never felt deprived. It seemed that all my friends were in similar situations. Later, I may have felt that I missed out on some things and would want to do better for my children, but I never felt disadvantaged.

My wife Yvonne's experiences in growing up led to developing her own awareness and assertion of independence. Her parents immigrated to the United States in their youth, and their social life involved interaction with friends born in their native region of Piedmont, Italy. Ines and Lorenzo were self-conscious about their use of English and talked to Yvonne only in the dialect of Piedmont. Her exposure to foreign tongues continued when Ines returned to work and her grandmother, who spoke only the Piedmont dialect and French, came over from Italy to take care of Yvonne. Yvonne started learning English when she entered kindergarten and, being a good student, she learned quickly. Most of her girlfriends came from very similar backgrounds, so she had a minimal exposure to what was a typical city environment. However, her curiosity to expand her interests led to her becoming an avid reader and excelling in an advanced accelerated high school program that led to her acceptance at Queens College. Her parents had little empathy and support for her college aspirations, and after two years Yvonne went to work. My parents gave me some support in helping with my education, but Yvonne's parents were more interested in seeing that she married a nice boy from Piedmont like her friends had done. Fitting into the American culture was something Yvonne had to accomplish by herself.

We got married when I was twenty-five and Yvonne was only twenty. We didn't waste too much time in raising a family; after less than five years we had three children—Susan, the oldest; Larry, two years younger; and Ray, just eighteen months later. They were so cute, and hugging and kissing them was so natural and pleasurable. I was not able to recall similar physical demonstrations with my parents. Maybe they stopped these affectionate expressions at an earlier age than I could remember. Yvonne and I lived first in a three-bedroom house in the suburbs with a big backyard to play in. There was a hill to slide down in winter and a clump of trees and bushes to hide out with your friends.

When Susan was almost six years old, the family left our typical suburban environment and crossed the Atlantic by boat to live with Yvonne's parents— who had planned a lengthy vacation in Italy—in a two-bedroom, one-bath apartment in Ivrea, Italy, while I went to work in remote eastern Turkey. Although her relatives in the area gave some support to Yvonne, she was the principal organizer of family activities. In a period of seven months, I got to see the family twice; each time I delighted in seeing their adaptation to Italian surroundings. The Italian people are so taken with children, and a large family with such a young mother caused much admiration and expressions of delight. How could you not smile when a cute two-year-old American boy goes into the dining room of a hotel and greets the diners with a loud "Buona Sera"?

The children don't remember much, if anything, of their stay in Italy. But on our return, Susan's first-grade teacher commented to Yvonne how mature Susan appeared in comparison to her classmates. She and Larry attended an Italian preschool for a little while, and Yvonne took all the children on short trips and visits to some relatives, so they were exposed to Italian culture. I guess it must be true what they say about travel broadening your mind and having a positive effect, so although the children don't remember much about living in Ivrea, the experience may have given them a good start in life.

Soon after returning from Italy, we moved into a larger house in a newly developing neighborhood with growing families. The children were beginning to emerge from requiring our constant attention, and it also became easier to get them involved in helping around the house and to expose them to interesting activities and holidays. It seemed almost too soon afterward that they started to pursue their own individual pastimes.

The first Christmas after we moved into our new house, Yvonne and I went out and bought skiing equipment and clothes for everyone. Skiing became an activity that developed into a passion for the whole family and gave us many years of quality time together. I felt compelled to write an extensive picture of this facet of our lives and I share it with you later.

In trying to get my boys involved with what Daddy was doing, I may have begun too early having them help with chores. I set out to build a large deck in our backyard, and I needed one-by-twelve-foot supporting beams to hold the redwood flooring boards. At the time, weather-treated joist lumber wasn't available, so I decided that I would treat the wood with creosote. I got a couple of big buckets of the material and two brushes for my underage boys to spread it on each beam. They thought it was great fun, and then I noticed after they had swabbed several boards their bare legs were turning red. I then realized that the material was very corrosive, and I washed their legs with water and put some cream on their skin. They were brave boys and didn't cry, and they said it felt like sunburn. I limited their future assistance on my project to helping move boards around and watching what I was doing.

As the boys grew older, I introduced them to the use of snow shovels; in Syracuse I appreciated sharing the chore of shoveling with them. I eventually bought a snowblower to make snow removal a lot easier. Later, I used the boys' muscles to help till the soil and remove the weeds from our vegetable garden. We had a big empty lot behind our house, and for years I used it to raise food for our table. We spent time in the fall canning and freezing the bounty of our garden. For two years this last task involved the whole family contributing because I became ambitious and planted several rows of corn. We had enough plants to yield 300 ears of corn, and it all reached maturity at about the same time. Everyone had a task in harvesting this crop. The corn was husked and then parboiled; kernels were stripped off the cob and finally bagged for freezing. With everybody helping, we completed the job in one day. Thank goodness everyone liked corn; the ratatouille we canned was not as popular.

An amusing incident occurred as we tried to protect our crop from some pesky groundhogs. One year I contracted with a neighbor's son to trap one, but the following year I decided to get rid of the critter by myself. I located the animal's tunnel and bought a poisonous smoke bomb. Ray was with me when we set out about our messy task. We had accumulated some rocks to block the tunnel entrance, and after igniting the bomb, we quickly trapped the animal. However, it wasn't going to pass away easily, and it started to try and push away the rocks. We became a bit fearful that our plan would fail, but Ray quickly grabbed a shovel and held the rocks in place until the groundhog finally gave up. Ray was proud of his triumph and to this day still recalls the incident.

In my front yard were two large pear trees that required my attention. In the spring, the trees were briefly filled with beautiful white flowers and budding leaves. During the summer, we had ripening pears and shade for our house. However, in the fall, harvesting or disposing of the pears became a frustrating and messy activity. I tried making wine or sauce with the fruit and gave away some to whoever wanted any. However, the harvest was always too abundant, and most of the pears wound up in the garbage. Collecting the droppings for disposal was a problem, and one year I thought I had a smart idea to involve the boys in the process. I offered them a penny for each pear they picked up, but pretty soon so many had fallen that I lowered my wages to a penny for every four pears. The boys' visions of getting rich diminished and they became less interested, so I had to again pitch in. A couple years later I had the trees taken down and planted one that only provided shade.

We tried to get our children involved around the house, and although their allowances weren't large, we did compensate for their help by taking them on some fun holidays. During the winter we took them to Vermont and the Adirondacks for skiing weekends, and in the summer we went to camps and resorts along the east coast to escape our usual routine. On one ambitious trip we spent a week at Myrtle Beach before making a visit to Disneyland. We all had a wonderful time, and years later when Yvonne and I returned by ourselves, we realized how important it was to have children along to enjoy this mecca of a tourist attraction.

Although we always went on exciting vacations, we really gave our children an exceptional experience ten years after they returned from living in Italy. At the time I had the responsibility to develop technical interaction with Italian aerospace companies. I had made two trips to Italy, and one more visit during the summer was in my plans. I was entitled to several weeks of vacation, and I decided to combine my business trip with a tour of Europe with my family. After the children's school year ended, we all got on a plane for Italy, landing in Rome. While I attended business meetings, my family visited St. Peter's Cathedral, threw coins in the Fountain of Trevi, walked about the Coliseum, and strolled through many of Rome's famous streets. I had previously visited many of the places, and I was happy just sharing an evening meal with them in several wonderful Italian restaurants.

I rented a car and drove to Florence by way of a lunch in Orvieto. I only had one meeting in this city, so I could spend more time roaming this art-filled place with my family. The children weren't overly enthusiastic about the Uffizi Museum, but they couldn't help but be impressed by the David sculpture.

My plans called for taking the children to stay with Yvonne's parents in the village of Vestigne while she accompanied me to LaSpezzia and Milano, where I had meetings to attend. Her fluency with the language allowed her to enjoy wandering about Italian cities by herself. When we returned to the village, the grandparents' courtyard was filled with children who were attracted to socializing with Americans. One day we went on a hike in the Alps with some friends from Vestigne, and on the weekend we took the children to the mountain ski village of Cervinia to ski on the huge glacier that is in the shadow of the massive Matterhorn peak (Cervino in Italian).

In spite of Larry breaking his finger soon after we arrived, the following day was filled with experiences we can never forget. The sky was a bright blue, with no clouds to mask the white peaks that surrounded us. The steep rocky slopes of the Matterhorn were snowless, which made the mountain look even more awesome. We skied on the gentle slopes of the glacier, absorbing the beauty of nature about us until the sun softened the surface of the snow. With ravenous appetites we returned to our hotel to eat a hardy meal. Afterward, with the sun still bright and warm, we lounged on a patio and enjoyed a restful siesta. It seemed that day that so many of our sensory needs were satisfied, and it made us all look forward to coming back the next day before returning to Vestigne to prepare for leaving Italy.

It took awhile to leave because we had to say good-bye to so many people, and each social call required sharing a drink, exchange of kisses, and lengthy best wishes for a bon voyage. We left with our little Fiat packed with five people, suitcases, and things we had bought or were given. Late in the afternoon we arrived at Zurich, our next destination, where the children learned about eating raclette and the Swiss's substitute for the seashore, a wave machine. We were heading for Paris, but we took our time getting there, stopping in Strasbourg and a town just outside of the city. The problem when we entered Paris was finding the drop-off office for the car. We were going to return to Syracuse from London, but we were planning on using public transportation for the rest of our journey. Yvonne's knowledge of French managed to obtain information for us to find the rental car office. However, in my struggle to follow directions, I had to negotiate the world's widest traffic circle, around the Arch of Triumph; getting rid of the car allowed me to relax and enjoy Paris.

There is so much of the city's charm that you can take pleasure in by walking and riding the subway. We spent three days in Paris and saw all its well-known sights. We let the children roam the streets near the hotel by themselves, and Susan got a chance to use her high school French when she bought ice cream and ordered breakfast for her and the boys. Yvonne and I even got away by ourselves for a nightclub tour.

We left Paris by a train that went to a port that was a launching point for a hydrofoil. At the time this was the quickest way to cross the English Channel. The hydrofoil is more like a plane than a boat, since the cabin contains plane-like chairs with seat belts and stewards to give you directions. The roar of the engine rivals that of a jet, but once you hit water, the roughness of the channel sea makes the journey feel like a high-speed ride on a washboard; the voyage was unique.

London was cloudy and rainy, but like the stoic English we tried to ignore the weather. We went to the Tower of London to see the royal jewels and noted the past horrors that took place in its dungeons. A visit to Windsor Castle showed the splendor of royal life. We dined at the elegant Simpson's restaurant, where the boys were given ties to wear while eating their roast beef and Yorkshire pudding. Our visit was somewhat spoiled because the excessive mold all about us caused Larry's asthma to greatly affect his breathing. However, an hour after takeoff, he became his usual healthy self again.

We reflected on the trip for many years, and all the experiences we shared brought us closer together as a family and instilled in everyone the zeal for travel.

Although we did a lot of things together with the children, when they entered school they all started to pursue some of their own interests. They were encouraged to play musical instruments, so each of them tested their attraction for music. Susan started playing the flute, but when entering high school switched to bassoon to play in the orchestra and the sax to play in the marching band. She even considered pursuing music in college. Larry started playing the trumpet and Ray the drums, but as soon as they became involved in competitive sports, they lost interest.

The boys' first venture into sports occurred with their competing in the punt, pass, and kick contests sponsored by the Ford Motor Company. For two years they each won their first round of competition, and if they could have combined Larry's passing ability with Ray's kicking skill, they might have gone all the way. I enjoyed being the pass receiver and kick returner as they practiced. I got involved coaching them in Little League baseball and Kiwanis basketball, and when they entered high school their skill in sports led them both to have noteworthy accomplishments playing football and basketball. In fact, Division 1A colleges recruited them to play football, and both wound up taking part in this sport for Bucknell University until injuries ended their careers.

While the children were attending high school, we were kept busy supporting participation in all their activities. Susan kept us the most busy because she was involved in so many things. She had band competitions, orchestra recitals, synchronous swim contests, and gymnastic meets, while the boys limited themselves to football and basketball. It was fun and time passed too quickly.

It was obvious that our relationship with our children was quite different than Yvonne or I had experienced with our parents. But the associations probably weren't much different than many of our neighbors and friends. The effect on a child's development can be evaluated only after they leave home. Each child has had a flourishing professional career, and each has had a successful marriage that has blessed us with nine loving grandchildren. Although large distances now separate us, we try to maintain a caring attachment with some yearly visits and weekly phone calls. You might say we are proud and fortunate parents.

AN OFFBEAT PATH THROUGH COLLEGE

Unfolding the story of my rather unconventional passage through college describes a somewhat different way of obtaining a degree

Back when I got out of high school, things were quite different. World War II had ended, defense plants were closing down, and GIs were flocking into the colleges and the job market. It was time for me to jump into this somewhat chaotic environment and embark on some kind of career path. Going to college was not something I grew up anticipating. My parents' resources made going to a private college out of the question, and since I did not take a language while attending high school, I lacked a requirement to attend a free New York City college. I had received a rather advanced electrical technology education at the very competitive Brooklyn Technical High School, and I expected that I would be qualified for some interesting kind of work. However, my attempts at employment uncovered nothing of interest to me, and I was quite discouraged. Someone gave me information about a junior college that had opened a year earlier that offered a basic engineering course. It was a work-cooperative school run by the YMCA and promised employment and interesting jobs after each three-month semester. I applied for admittance and was told they would let me know.

My father became concerned that I would spend the summer hanging out on the street corner, so he sent me to see a friend who ran a garment factory. My father said, "I am sure he can find something to keep you busy. Besides, who knows if the college will accept you, and maybe the job can offer you some longer-term employment."

I wasn't excited about the opportunity but I decided I needed some money, so off I went to seek my fortune. The place was a small factory building located on the outskirts of Queens, New York. Inside were long tables where men were cutting fabric into the pieces of a women's suit. Next to them were women sewing the pieces into bigger pieces and passing them on to women who were forming the suit jackets and skirts. Nearby were the pressers, flattening seams and taking the wrinkles out of the fabric. At the end of my tour, I said to my father's friend, "What can I do around here?"

"Well, I need help with a lot of little chores that need doing around here. It will be a chance for you to learn how a place like this operates. The job pays $20 a week."

My father must have talked to the man. I didn't say it, but I thought, he's looking for a gofer. I did say, "It sounds like it might be an interesting job." For the next four weeks I conscientiously applied myself to the work. It did turn out to be an appealing job because I got to know everybody in the place. Everyone treated me like a young family member since I was the newest person in the factory. The head presser had been doing his job for twenty years, while a man ten years his junior was just starting out as a presser; he was trying to support a wife and two children on $25 a week. It was surprising how easy it was to develop rapport with everyone.

I soon found out I was accepted at the junior college and felt relieved that there would be a different career opportunity in my future. I told the boss I would be leaving at the end of the summer and asked if it would be possible for me to have a higher-paying job as a presser. He said, "You have worked hard and deserve a raise." I soon found myself working beside the father of two children. I noticed that after standing all day on a concrete floor with only a break at lunch, my young legs were extremely tired and walking to the subway caused a lot of discomfort. I gained a lot of respect for the other men who stood with me.

There was an incident that got me notoriety and caused great embarrassment. One hot summer day the radio that was on all day stopped working. I told the boss I had some knowledge of electricity and maybe I could fix the radio. I was taking it apart when I accidently caused an electrical short circuit and all the fans that were keeping the place livable stopped. My embarrassment turned to panic when I realized no one knew where the fuse box was located. That night the maintenance people got things back to normal, and from that day on I was known as young Tom Edison. I am sure many people thought this young man had a lot to learn at college.

The college had only about 200 students and was called Walter Hervey. Its liberal arts classrooms were housed in a building attached to one of the country's largest YMCAs, located on West 63rd Street a couple of hundred feet from Central Park West . A walk down to 20th Street and 9th Avenue, a distance of 2.5 miles, brought you to the engineering classrooms and laboratories. The engineering students were sure to be in shape when they graduated. Taking buses was not a convenient option.

The teachers were quite competent, and Dr. Carl Hammer was one who was particularly outstanding; he was a math professor who received his doctorate from the University of Munich. During his lectures I was always left with the feeling that I understood what he was trying to teach me. Besides giving well-organized lectures, he applied techniques from the old country by giving term projects in mathematics. He tried to teach precision and accuracy by assigning problems that required the use of 12-place logs and trig tables to get the right answers. In advanced algebra he gave out problems where several complex equations were necessary for a solution. For calculus, you had to take derivatives and do integrations of very complicated mathematical expressions. He got me so interested in the subject that I considered becoming a math teacher.

Four times for three months I left the academic environment to join the working world. The jobs were quite varied and some were even interesting. I was employed by Coca Cola to work in what they called their engineering department. It was really a testing lab to verify the durability of soda vending machines, bottling crates, and six-pack cartons. It had some interesting aspects, and I was never thirsty. Another time I worked in the test laboratory of a chemical plant that made cleaning products. Chemists sampled the production at different stages to ensure quality. I sometimes had problems communicating with the man I assisted because his very heavy southern drawl and my New York City accent resulted in us repeating ourselves or guessing at what was said. However, our struggling to understand each other led to us becoming good friends. The least interesting job was working in a factory making small household products. I worked at various production-line stations and I maintained my interest by seeing how fast I could do the different tasks. Of course, I had to be careful not to upset my coworkers, who liked a more relaxed pace.

The most taxing and challenging job was my first assignment, to a company that repaired and installed television sets. At that time TV ownership was in its infancy, and program reception usually came via dipole antennas mounted on the roof. In Manhattan that could mean that the TV and the antenna could be separated by many, many floors. Wire guides installed along the outside wall of the building fed the TV cable down to the customer's apartment. The three networks operating in the city had transmitting antennas located on top of the Empire State building, but rotating the customer's antenna was required to achieve the best compromise for reception among the three stations. Two people using walkie-talkies were necessary in most cases to do the job, so an installation could be complicated and time-consuming.

One day, with the temperature hovering well below freezing, my crew leader and I had to do a TV installation on the third floor of a twenty-five-story apartment house. He said to me, "A young fellow like you should have no trouble keeping warm, so why don't you go on the roof and mount the antenna and I'll run the cable down the building." I didn't know that a young person's blood was warmer than his but I really had no choice, so off I went. I took the elevator to the top floor, but when I went outside I found the highest point on the roof was reached by a twenty-foot vertically-mounted steel ladder. When I finally got to the top I noticed the beautiful view, but also the biting cold wind. I had to drill holes into concrete to mount inserts for the bolts that would hold the brackets for the antenna. This action is not easily accomplished in subfreezing temperatures, when friction between the manual drill's bit and socket hardly existed.

I first cursed as I started drilling, and then as I got colder and more frustrated, I started praying. Finally, God came to my rescue and I finished mounting the antenna. I then pointed it toward the Empire State building and attached the cable going down to the apartment. It was too cold to stay up there any longer adjusting things. We were so high up I figured it wouldn't make any difference. When it came time to descend the steel ladder I realized my hands were numb, so to get down I had to wrap my arms around the ladder to hold on.

My return to feeling warm was helped by the hot coffee the customer gave me. Also, the ten-dollar tip he gave us to split showed he appreciated the effort we had made getting him a TV picture. Few installations were that difficult but each presented special problems that had to be overcome, so each day presented a different challenge.

The cooperative college work experience certainly accelerated my maturity. I got to tackle and successfully complete many different tasks, which gave me the confidence to take on new challenges. In addition, I was exposed to many personal interactions with a wide spectrum of people. These types of career experiences are really more important than specific work activities.

I thought about going to a teacher's college and majoring in math, but a wise professor at school counseled me that if I wanted to teach math I could always do it after getting an engineering degree, but the opposite approach was not possible. Taking his advice, I enrolled at New York University's College of Engineering. I went from attending a small private college to matriculating at the country's largest private university. However, the engineering school and a small arts and science school were located on a 3000-student campus on the west side of the Bronx. The place had green lawns, an impressive quadrangle, dormitories, and fraternities. It was a small college nestled into a big city. I traveled three-quarters of an hour each way from my home in Queens to attend school, but I didn't mind because I used the time to do some of my homework.

I did well at school, participated in some campus activities, and joined a fraternity; I had become a typical college student, so I thought. However, some of my dates were a bit bizarre. I often took my father's car to pick up a date in Brooklyn and drove up the West Side Drive to attend a fraternity party in the Bronx. I had to return over the same route, so after twice visiting four of the five city boroughs I arrived home in the wee hours of the morning. After years of riding the subways and driving in the city, I took such a journey in stride and didn't think it was so unusual.

All my credits at the junior college were accepted at NYU, but over the summer I had to take a couple of sophomore courses that were prerequisites for my junior year. This meant no work and no money for summer amusement. I became desperate and learned that the Red Cross paid well for a pint of blood. I stood in line with some seedy characters, and though I was embarrassed the money made my summer more enjoyable.

During my senior year I had taken several job interviews on campus and had accepted an offer from General Electric to work for them. However, along came one of those life-changing occurrences that you have no way of anticipating. After I finished one of my final examinations, the chairman of the electrical engineering department offered me a fellowship to obtain a master's degree. I was flattered and had some personal reasons for not leaving the city, so I accepted his offer. It paid my tuition and awarded me $1500 of spending money; I never had had so much wealth.

In one year I had my degree, so after six years attending college I was finally ready to again face the outside world. It was a long and circuitous path, but I felt proud of my accomplishment. In completing this saga, I have a couple of noteworthy happenings to end my story. Years later I took my two teenage sons to visit the junior college I attended and found it no longer existed. I went next door to the YMCA and asked a very elderly man, who I assumed had been around a long time, what had happened to the school. He gave me a strange look and said, "I never heard of the place." The answer gave me a strange feeling, and my sons must have wondered if Dad was dreaming about his past. About the same time a piece appeared in the newspaper that NYU's College of Engineering was combining with Brooklyn Polytechnic Institute to form New York Poly Tech. In addition, the Bronx campus was being sold to the city and was to become the home for a community college. So I became a man without a college. For years New York Poly tried to get me to make donations, but I didn't even know what their campus looked like. The schools are gone, but not the fond memories of my college days.

WRITING MAKES FONDNESS GROW INTO LOVE

*Letter writing during my courtship helped me
to make a marriage commitment.*

We are all familiar with the idea that absence makes the heart grow fonder, but fondness is not love. Love requires more than a longing. It involves sharing ideas and thoughts and embracing them so that longing leads to attachment. Writing is a great way to bring out your inner self and express your feelings. In courting my wife, writing became the means that made it possible for me to propose and have our relationship grow prior to our marriage.

Finding or discovering one's soul mate, leading to a lifetime commitment, often seems directed by some guiding force. I know in my case that this was true, although at the time I had no inkling I was being guided.

I was at a dance hall in the borough of Queens with two friends. I often frequented the place on Saturday nights, but this time I felt the urge to do something different. I said to my friends, "We have been here many times. Why don't we try something different for a change? I understand they have some big dances in the city at the Manhattan Center." Without too much hesitation, they said, "Okay, let's go."

After a short subway ride we arrived at our destination and were surprised at how large the place was. Two dances were taking place, and it took us awhile to decide which looked the most interesting. We settled on a function being sponsored by an Italian organization. (I guess we were attracted to Italian women.) After wandering around, I spotted this very attractive young lady sitting with two friends. It must have been my lucky night because when I asked her to dance she said, "Yes."

Yvonne was her name. That was the start of a lovely evening and several months of dating. We were obviously attracted to one another, but at the time I was attending graduate school and preparing to get a job so a long-term commitment was far from my mind. Saying goodnight after a date included a lot of hugs and kisses, but little verbal expression of one's feelings.

Then one night Yvonne surprised me with some interesting but unwelcome news: she was planning to continue her college studies at the University of Turin in Italy. She was pleased and excited about her decision and I knew it was a great opportunity for her, but I was quite disappointed. I felt our relationship was probably going to end soon; after all, out of sight out of mind. However, we did agree to write to one another. I avoided seeing Yvonne off at the boat, which I found out later was a great letdown for her. I wasn't ready for a long-distance romance and I had a lot of uncertainty about what I wanted to do with my own future, so I was guarded in expressing too much interest.

It didn't take me long to begin missing Yvonne, and I wasn't sure when I would hear from her. After three weeks her first letter arrived, and it was filled with a description of the wonderful time she had with several young people also making the Atlantic crossing. She wondered if I still remembered her. I now knew that I had made a big mistake by not being more attentive when she left. I immediately sat down and wrote, trying to make amends for my behavior. It was frustrating to realize that it might be weeks before I received a reply.

I decided that waiting for her reply was too long a delay before expressing myself, so in a couple of days I wrote again to show that I missed her. She was pleased to receive my second letter and she didn't wait before writing again. So began a chain of letters across the ocean.

I enjoyed the time I spent alone with my thoughts and trying to express myself. In our early letters we gradually became a bit more expressive. At first I would sign off with a very polite "sincerely," and then I progressed to an affectionate "love." We started to say things to each other that we never said when saying goodnight after a date. For Christmas we had the perfect gift for each other: professional photographs.

When her picture arrived, I thought Yvonne had gotten even prettier. I now had even more inspiration for my writing sessions. I began to believe that this was the woman for me to marry. However, I wasn't sure when we would see each other again.

Months earlier I notified my draft board I wasn't going to apply for another occupational deferment. I found living my life in six-month intervals to be upsetting, and I was ready to fulfill my selective service obligation. They readily accepted my decision and requested my presence at Fort Dix in early April.

After Yvonne's first semester at the university, she had second thoughts about continuing her education abroad. The totally unstructured nature of her courses left her feeling dissatisfied about what she was learning. Soon after I told her I was being drafted, she wrote that she would be returning in early March. I was ecstatic, but concerned about the short window of overlap we had to see each other. To take full advantage of our time together, I was at the dock when her boat arrived.

On our very first date I proposed, using words that I knew were awkward. I felt that in a letter I would have been much more eloquent. Yvonne was somewhat surprised by my eagerness, but my letters had given some indication of my intentions. Her hesitant acceptance was followed by a few weeks of ardent dating, and our written expressions of affection became vocal demonstrations of our love.

After finding each other, we were now faced with parting again and using the written word to continue our relationship. During my time of basic training at Fort Dix in New Jersey, she managed to come down one Sunday when we recruits were given a day to ourselves. On another Sunday I managed to escape the base to meet her at the house of a family friend. Otherwise, the only link we had with each other was again through our letters.

After completing my training I was told I was being sent to Fort Bliss in El Paso, Texas, a long way from New York City. Again, my only connection with Yvonne was to be through the written word. In between expressions of longing for each other, we discussed plans for our future together.

I had been assigned by the army to be an instructor at a school for training soldiers to maintain radar-controlled anti-aircraft guns. Many of the instructors were college graduates who were married and living off the post. I thought that was a lifestyle change that was appealing. I suggested to Yvonne that we should take such a step. She readily agreed, but her mother couldn't understand why we were in such a rush. Finally our wishes prevailed and arrangements started to be made. We exchanged many letters after I suggested getting married, and I became discouraged by how long everything was taking. I had arrived in El Paso in July, and one year later I was finally returning home for the first time—to get married. Our correspondence filled a couple of shoe boxes and represented many hours of sharing very personal thoughts.

Unfortunately, our premarital experiences weren't the last time that letters were needed to ease the pain of absence. Eight years after getting married I had to spend six months working in remote eastern Turkey, and writing again became the bond that strengthened our love. I will always have a fondness for the written word.

Surviving an Army Fiasco

Dealing with a processing snafu immediately after entering the service gave an interesting start to my army career.

After graduating from college during the Korean War with a master's degree in electrical engineering, I got a job with a defense contractor, which enabled me to receive two six-month draft deferments. However, measuring my future in six-month intervals convinced me I needed a career change. Uncle Sam gladly accepted my offer to fulfill my military obligation, and I soon received my draft notification. I had learned that draftees with technical college degrees were put into assignments that tried to use their professional skills, so I was hoping to gain some worthwhile experience.

I reported to Fort Dix, New Jersey, and at the end of my first day in the army, I spent the night on KP, cutting up chickens for over a thousand men who had to be fed the next day. I began to have second thoughts about the valuable experience I was going to get in the army. The next two days I was left alone, and I and hundreds of other draftees were given a battery of written tests.

At the end of the testing period I noticed several men, who I knew had technical degrees like me, were called aside and given some paperwork to fill out. I went over and talked to them, and I found out they were being processed to go into to a scientific and professional pool. I became concerned that I wasn't included with them, and I wondered why. Nearby there was a sergeant who had been monitoring and supervising the testing, so I went over to him and said, "Sergeant, those men over there told me they were going to be put into a special assignment category for technical personnel after basic training. My education background is the same as theirs, and I wondered why I wasn't receiving the same processing."

He gave me a puzzled look. "What are you talking about? What special assignment?"

"I have an engineering degree, and I understand the army has special duty for these types of people."

"Oh, now I understand. It's an MOS [Military Occupational Specialty] called Scientific and Technical Personnel. You think you qualify?"

"Yes, I have the required educational requirements and some work experience. Could you please find out why I am being overlooked?"

He left and went into an office where they were processing the results, and after several minutes he returned. His explanation shocked me. "Soldier, you have the right educational credentials, but it seems your grade on the technical comprehension test was below the required level."

"There must be some mistake. I remember that test and it was quite simple. What can I do about this situation?"

"Well, you can write a complaint to the commanding general in Washington."

"You have to be kidding. The Korean War will be over by the time I receive a reply. Isn't there anything else I can do?"

"You can say you weren't feeling well and ask to take a retest."

This seemed like a helpful suggestion that might achieve some positive results, so I went off and submitted my request.

When I arrived at my basic training company I found out that there was another person named D'Amico in the group and his first name was Vincent. Since my name was Victor, I began to understand how the test scores might have gotten mixed up. Vincent was a farm boy who had not finished high school. After four weeks of basic training and no response to my request, I began to wonder if anyone was paying attention to my predicament. Finally, after five weeks, I was summoned to take the test again. I breezed through the exam and was allowed to hang around to find out about the result.

An officer came out to speak to me and said, "We have never seen such a dramatic change in a test result before. You certainly qualify for an S&P MOS rating."

I was so relieved that I didn't bother to try and explain what might have happened. I now had a much more positive attitude toward my basic training. I had one more anxious moment at the end of my instruction when people were being told where they were going next. My processing had obviously been delayed since I had not received any orders. I was just hanging around, hoping no one would think it would be a good idea to send me on to the next eight weeks of advanced basic training. Fortunately, no one had such a bright idea and I was soon told to get on a plane and go to the Army's anti-aircraft school at Fort Bliss in El Paso, Texas.

Except for the fact that I had to pull KP once in a while, Fort Bliss was a fine place to spend my enlisted career in the army. For almost two years I taught enlisted men and officers about the operation and maintenance of radars that controlled the firing of anti-aircraft guns. After I left the service, my experience made it easy for me to get a job with a defense contractor that was a leading supplier of military radars.

I have often wondered what my military career would have been had I not asserted myself during those first days in the army. Trying to cope and find your way in such a large organization can be an overwhelming experience.

The Start of Marriage

After a long separation came an auspicious beginning to living together.

Shortly after Yvonne accepted my marriage proposal, I entered the army and our letter-writing courtship began again. For two months we were only a few hours away from each other and saw one another on two occasions. But after basic training the army sent me thousands of miles away to be an instructor at a school in El Paso, Texas. Now letters and an occasional phone call were our only means of contact, and it was difficult to imagine when we would see each other again.

After I settled into my new lifestyle, I noted that there were several new instructors like myself who brought their wives with them and were living off the post. When I told Yvonne and suggested that in a little while we could get married, she thought it was a good idea. Unfortunately the little while became a long while. First, Yvonne's grandmother got gravely ill, and Yvonne and her mother spent several months in Italy trying to comfort her. After arriving home in January, she tried to make wedding arrangements and found that getting dates for the church and reception were difficult. It wasn't until the middle of July that everything could be set up. So, one year after leaving home, I boarded a plane to return.

I planned to arrive home only three days before the wedding, since I was trying to conserve leave time for our honeymoon and the long car ride back to El Paso. Yvonne had taken care of most of the preparations, and my main responsibility was to buy a car for our trip. I had never owned a car; living in the city, owning a car is not a necessity, and when it was convenient, I would often be able to borrow my father's car. With the money I had saved working before I went into the army, I was able to buy a one-year-old Chevrolet. We had impressive plans for our honeymoon. Our intent was to travel down the east coast to Miami, Florida, where Yvonne had a good family friend who had extended us an invitation to stay at a rooming house he ran. Then we were going to visit another friend in Pensacola before heading west to El Paso. I joined the American Automobile Association and got trip tickets that outlined the whole journey. For someone who had never driven beyond the environs of New York City, it was an ambitious undertaking; it shows the bravado of youth, especially since Yvonne did not yet know how to drive.

My twenty-year-old bride-to-be, with little help from her parents, did a wonderful job of arranging the wedding. She had bought our wedding bands, rented my formal wear, sent out the invitations, made plans for the limousines, reserved the church, ordered the flowers, selected the hotel and the menu for the reception, and even reserved a room for our wedding night.

All the preparations led to a splendid day in which everyone had a wonderful time. The only negative moment occurred when Yvonne and I returned to her parents' apartment. We had dropped off our wedding attire, put some gifts and our suitcases in the car, and were preparing to leave for the hotel. It was time to say goodbye, and when I couldn't call Ines "Mama" she broke into tears. I was surprised at her reaction, but somehow I just couldn't do it at the moment. It wasn't a great start and it took time to get over the awkward situation, but we eventually developed a relationship where I truly became the son she never had. In fact, when she came to live with us, the relationship became in many ways as deep and warm as with my own mother.

We left New York and our first stop was Washington; there I got my first glimpse of our nation's capital. Neither of us remembers much about that visit, but we both never forgot the wonderful meal at a fine restaurant with tuxedo-clad waiters who kept addressing Yvonne as "ma'am." My young wife was flattered and felt so grown-up.

There were no superhighways traveling south at that time, and it took awhile to reach Miami. The rooming house of the family friend was a modest place, and our room had twin beds on opposite walls. It obviously wasn't a place for honeymooners, so we quickly made reservations at a hotel on the beach. We spent two nights at the rooming house and slept in one bed but made sure the other was messed up.

After two days of enjoying the luxury of the hotel and the warm sunny beach, we were ready to leave. However, Yvonne experienced two incidents that left her with some unpleasant memories. First, our time on the beach gave her a rather unpleasant sunburn, which took several days to heal. Then, as we were leaving the hotel, the doorman closed the car door on her finger. The height of gall occurred when after the doorman's blunder, he held out his hand for a tip. Fortunately, an ice pack relieved some of the discomfort and a doctor's attention wasn't necessary. The incidents prompted me to give Yvonne some extra tender loving care.

My friend, Neil, in Pensacola had just recently been married; they were in the process of furnishing their house and didn't have great accommodations for guests. The night we spent with them, we slept on a mattress placed on the floor. Neil's wife took Yvonne shopping for a wedding gift, and the blanket and pot they bought were household fixtures for many years.

Our next extended stop was New Orleans, a city that our tour book said had a lot to offer. We booked into a hotel near the French Quarter and spent two days exploring that charming and exciting place. Strolling through Jackson Square, we bought two unusual black and white paintings that hung upon our house walls for many years. We enjoyed an expensive but elegant meal at Antoine's, a restaurant whose reputation was legend.

Leaving New Orleans, we were faced with traveling across the vast expanse of Texas leading to El Paso. We all know Texas is a big state, but driving across it makes it seem even bigger. We spent almost three days getting to El Paso and were on roads where we seldom saw a car. We would drive for hours heading toward mountains that never seemed to get any closer. Two days after arriving in El Paso I got a flat tire, and when I went to fix it I found that the spare was flat. I couldn't help thinking of the awful predicament we would have been in had the flat occurred on some of the desolate roads I had been driving on.

Before leaving for New York I had made arrangements with an army buddy, a part-time superintendent at an apartment house in El Paso, to rent a small furnished apartment. "Small" might have been an exaggeration; it had one room that contained a bed, a dresser, and a small area with some living-room furniture, a tiny kitchen with eating space for two people, and a bathroom. It wasn't much, but Yvonne made it into a cozy place. She got her mother to make some drapes and a bedspread, bought some colorful doilies to scatter around, and purchased a screen to separate the sleeping area from the living room. Visitors commented on how charming it looked.

Yvonne got a sales job at the White House, the nicest department store in the city, which was within walking distance of our apartment. Her experience working at Bonwit Teller in New York City impressed the employment personnel. We both worked six days a week, but I had Wednesday and Saturday afternoon off, so on Wednesdays I did the wash and on Saturdays I made dinner.

To give us some time to socialize, we were able to hire a Mexican woman to do the ironing and clean the house. When she came to work, Yvonne would make the long uphill climb to our apartment during her lunch hour to pay her and make sure there were no problems. Yvonne's coworkers thought she was a bit crazy to make that trek during the midday El Paso heat.

Dick, my upper bunkmate for a year and a very good friend, got married three weeks after me. His bride, Nancy, was older than Yvonne and had worked a year teaching in a grammar school. We all spent a lot of our time together and our wives became good friends. Going across the border to Juarez, as a bachelor, was often a favorite activity, but with our wives, it wasn't as popular. The nightclub shows in Juarez could be embarrassing for the ladies and their restaurant food was not particularly good, so we stayed on our side of the border. One of our favorite pastimes was teaching the ladies how to play bridge. I played with Nancy as my partner and Dick played with Yvonne, so we never had any arguments. When we first played cards with them, Nancy, who had some experience entertaining, prepared a nice dessert for us. Of course, Yvonne had to reciprocate and her limited culinary skills were tested, but a basic *Better Homes and Gardens* cookbook helped her meet the challenge.

In order to host the bridge game at our apartment, we had to buy a folding card table and chairs, and with this purchase, we also were able to invite people to eat at our home. One unforgettable dinner was our first Thanksgiving together when we asked my good friend, Lyle, to share the meal with us. At that time Yvonne was skittish about touching the turkey's flesh, so she dressed and prepared the turkey using two forks. Lyle never noticed that the human touch was missing from the meal.

Liquor was cheap in Juarez: a gallon of gin could be bought for $2.50, so many of the couples would have parties on Saturday nights and martinis were the favorite beverage. Small apartments and large crowds made them noisy, but comfy, events. We labored long hours, but the work was not stressful and weekends were always a time for relaxing. Most of the instructors were graduate engineers, and there were so many of us that we formed an engineering organization and held several meetings. It made us feel like professionals again.

We met many people who were all in similar situations, recently married with our lives somewhat on hold, fulfilling our draft responsibility. When I was discharged and it was time to leave, I realized that our months in El Paso were somewhat of a unique opportunity and a positive way to start our marriage. We were free of family connections and responsibility and had to rely on each other, but we had many friends who made life interesting and fun.

Our relationship with Dick and Nancy became close, and we continued to correspond and occasionally visit each other for several years until a tragedy occurred. After the birth of their second child, we heard Nancy was having some problems. Then one day we were shocked when Dick sent us a telegram saying that "we have lost our beloved Nancy." An army friend we knew who worked with Dick told us Nancy had been suffering from postpartum depression and had taken her life. It was the most upsetting and stunning experience Yvonne and I have ever encountered. Neither of us, at that time, had ever experienced the loss of a person close to us, and it was devastating. It was hard for us to imagine, depression causing one to take such drastic action. This tragic moment made our memory of those early days of our marriage with Nancy and Dick so very poignant.

Passage from Student to Teacher

*Learning to instruct in the army and then building on
this experience enabled me to lecture in college.*

We all have spent time being students. It can be a very rewarding experience to learn, especially when you receive recognition for your knowledge or accomplishments. However, receiving negative feedback or correction of your learning activities can be even more instructive. I remember when I was quite young, my teacher tried to make me part of a class chorus. She listened to us for a while and politely turned to me and said, "Victor, why don't you just move your lips." I never forgot the guidance I was given, and when I am in church and hymns are being sung, only my lips will be moving. During my college years after several beers at a fraternity party, you could hear my off-key rendition of some old-time favorites.

I managed to learn enough in grammar school to gain entrance to a very competitive high school, where I distinguished myself by being an average student. However, I learned in my competitive scholastic environment that hard work was needed to achieve even modest success. This served me well when I went to college. Just prior to graduating I finally received some recognition for my labors by having the chairman of the electrical engineering department offer me a fellowship to obtain a master's degree.

After six years in college I was more than ready to leave the academic environment and enter the industrial world, but after a short professional career Uncle Sam showed me there was another milieu for me, the U.S. Army. They decided with my background I knew enough to teach at a school that taught men how to maintain the army's radar-controlled anti-aircraft guns. It was a complex system and required many weeks of training to become competent. The course was administered by a captain, assisted by a lieutenant, who assigned six instructors to teach the material. Three of us were enlisted men, and the other three were civilians working for RCA. Being a private, I was the lowest man on the pay scale, earning $90 a month, while RCA paid their people $150 a week. I really didn't resent this disparity because I felt being able to satisfy my selective service obligation and gain some valuable experience was worthwhile compensation.

The course was well organized. There were detailed lesson plans for the long three-hour lectures each morning before the students were taken out to become familiar with the equipment. I was expected to study the lesson plans and then amplify on the ideas presented and answer the questions raised. I found that giving a lecture was extremely tiring. You would pace up and down in the front of the classroom lecturing, writing on the blackboard, and answering questions. During the short breaks the students would approach you with all sorts of queries, and you never got a chance to sit down. I would return to the barracks at lunchtime and collapse on my bunk. I even lost my appetite on those days I was teaching. Conducting classes on the equipment was a lot less tiring and even fun to do. I would dream up problems to introduce into the system and be amused by the students' attempts to fix them.

I became knowledgeable about the course material and the equipment and was scheduled to go on somewhat of a boondoggle trip to test personnel at field sites around the country. The captain had second thoughts about offering me this plum of an assignment and decided it should be given to a regular army sergeant instructor. I was disappointed, but it was probably the right thing to do.

During my army career I learned a lot about radar, but probably more importantly I gained the poise to get up and talk before a group. When I received an early army release to take more college courses at my alma mater, I had the confidence to write and ask the department chairman if there were any classes I could assist in teaching. He had not forgotten me and told me to see him when I returned.

I arrived on campus a week before the start of the spring semester, and though it had been almost three years since I had left, everything seemed quite familiar. However, thinking I would now be a teacher instead of a student caused me some anxiety. The department chair gave me a friendly greeting and asked several questions about what I had been doing. He then said, "I am so glad you wrote me about wanting to teach because this semester I have some problems in handling the teaching workload."

I had envisioned helping out in a laboratory class, but he seemed to have something a little more challenging in mind.

"I need an instructor to teach two electrical courses to mechanical engineering students. One course is in electric circuitry, and the other is in AC/DC machinery. They are real basic courses and you should have no trouble with the material."

I was glad he had so much confidence in me. I had only taken one machinery course as an undergraduate, so I was feeling a little inadequate. I asked, "What plans do you have for the courses or what material do you want me to cover?"

He reached into a drawer and took out two textbooks and laid them on his desk. On top of one book he placed a single sheet of paper and said, "This is the outline and text for the circuitry course. The other book has been used by our electrical engineering students and we have no outline for teaching out-of-department students. You will have to study the material and simplify the information that you present."

I was flabbergasted. No, I was shocked. I couldn't help but think about all the guidance I was given for my classes in the army. I tried to hide my surprise and asked, "How many students are in the class and how many lectures will I have to give each week?"

"There are thirty students and three lecture sessions for each course. In addition, there is a laboratory class once a week."

My God, I was going to be one busy fellow. I was beginning to having second thoughts about offering my services. After a low-stress tour in the army, it was going to be a real challenge to plan for all these lectures and take two graduate courses. We discussed some other details about my responsibilities, but I was eager to leave and try to figure out what I would have to do to get ready.

I had one week to prepare for my first lecture. After studying the circuitry course text and outline, I felt comfortable with the material I had to teach. It contained ideas and theories I was quite familiar with. The machinery course was another matter. I could do only about half the problems in the textbook. The book was used by electrical engineering majors, and material was just too advanced for mechanical engineering students. I had some books at home that treated the subject in a more basic way, so I decided I would follow their approach. For each course I elected to prepare notes that kept me about two weeks ahead of the students.

After greeting my large class, I realized I had a motivational problem. These students were interested in heat transfer and strength of materials theory; electrical concepts were not of much interest to them. I remember later in the circuitry course trying to relate the theory to the flow of water through pipes in order to perk their interest. After a few weeks I started to feel at ease in the classroom. My army teaching experience was invaluable in getting me to use the blackboard properly and to solicit responses from the students. Although I was getting to feel good about what I was doing, I realized I had to find out if the students understood me.

As a student I realized taking a test can be a rather foreboding experience. However, I didn't appreciate that giving a test could also cause the teacher some apprehension. You had to make the questions challenging, cover the scope of the material you presented, and then wait to see if the students were meeting your expectations. It was a lot of work preparing an examination and just as much work correcting it. I remember when I graded my first test, I evaluated the partial credit I gave when I reviewed the first students' answers. As I noticed some of the same mistakes being made by other students, I became less critical, so I was more generous in awarding partial credit as I proceeded. I found that reviewing the total class without giving a grade made me more equitable in scoring the test. With thirty students in each class to evaluate, the whole process was quite time-consuming, and I was not eager to give examinations. So, both student and teacher can have an unenthusiastic attitude about examinations.

Laboratory classes presented a different set of challenges. Each experiment required the student to wire together equipment and then exercise it to obtain data. One of my duties was to inspect the students' wiring connections to make sure they had done it correctly. I was especially careful in doing this task because there was a danger to both the student and the equipment if any mistakes were made. One day a student grabbed the wrong end of a wire that he needed to reconnect in what was considered a simple step in an experiment. When he tried to reposition the wire, he put a dead short circuit across the laboratory generator. The result was a one-foot-long electrical arc, a loud pop of the circuit breaker opening, and the piercing noise of the generator slowing down. Needless to say, the young man was frightened and all of his classmates had a new respect for electricity. I thought maybe they would now pay more attention in class.

I was especially proud of my accomplishments in the machinery course. My limited knowledge of the subject made me more sensitive to the students' problems in understanding the material. I got very basic in my explanations, and their test results showed I was getting through to them. I had to flunk only one student in all my classes. His problem was the class was too early in the morning, so he missed a lot of the lectures.

My biggest disappointment from teaching in college was that no one seemed too interested in what I was doing. Nobody dropped by in my classes to observe or asked me any questions about my progress. The administration's chief concern was that I get the final grades in on time. I was basically on my own; as long as the students didn't complain, I was doing my job.

It was a job I look back on with a great deal of satisfaction. Facing sixty students each week with no guidance and such little time to prepare myself gave me confidence about addressing any future challenges I might encounter.

AN AMERICAN HOUSEWIFE LIVING IN ITALY

My wife's experiences in caring for our young family in Ivrea, Italy, were a confidence builder for her future.

Some years ago when my children were quite young, my job required me to go to remote eastern Turkey for several months to assist in the installation of a radar system. I was concerned about how my family and especially my wife would cope. Raising two- and four-year-old boys and a six-year-old girl is a difficult job even with a husband supporting you.

My in-laws, then retired, were planning to spend several months living in Ivrea, Italy, a town in which they had spent some of their youth. When they heard of our dilemma they gave my wife, Yvonne, an option that she immediately accepted. "Join us in Ivrea, and we can live together while your husband is away." It was a choice that was filled with problems, but as Yvonne told me, being with family offers a closeness that friends and neighbors cannot provide. Although I knew the key events that happened to her while she was living in Italy, it took me years to appreciate what she went through. Recent conversations with her gave me the insight to fully understand this period in her life. Her story is one where an independent spirit and the warmth and friendliness of Italians made for a wonderful family experience in spite of the problems encountered at times.

Yvonne was not a typical suburban housewife. She fluently spoke Italian and the Piedmont dialect and as a single woman had been to Ivrea on four occasions. However, she also had for many years become accustomed to the lifestyle of raising a family in upstate New York—a place where the help of friends substituted for family assistance and the conveniences of the American lifestyle were taken for granted.

After making arrangements to have a Volkswagen bug delivered in Italy, Yvonne set sail on the USS *Independence* with her parents and our three children. When the boat docked in Genoa, Cousin Angelo was there with his truck to meet everyone. They were all delivered to her aunt's small hotel in Ivrea, where they were to stay until other accommodations could be found. You see how nice it is to have family to lend some support.

Living in a one-star hotel with small rooms and without a private bath is not too pleasant, so Yvonne kept the kids outside a lot. Many people got to meet the children and enjoy their antics; they were really cute. Two folks who were charmed by the children and loved seeing them were Signore and Signora Rolla, who owned a gas station next door to the hotel. Their fondness for my family made them bestow their generosity on Yvonne. When Signore Rolla found out Yvonne had to go to Milan to pick up the Volkswagen we had bought, he felt it would be a difficult chore for her. After all, going to Italy's largest city and finding the car dealer and driving a new car with a stick shift on the floor was a formidable undertaking. So he went with a friend and brought the car to the hotel. It was the start of a wonderful friendship.

Angelo came to Yvonne's aid again when he found them a new apartment they could rent and helped them negotiate with a store to supply enough furniture to make it a comfortable place to live. The proprietor's sympathy for the family resulted in him making a bighearted offer to sell the furniture with an agreed price to buy it back when everybody left. So, two weeks after arriving, they were all settled into a new flat with a yard for the little inflatable pool Yvonne brought with her from the States and a new car for making getting around much easier. Yvonne had now acquired some of the essentials for facing life in Ivrea, a place quite different from home. However, she was still missing many of the amenities of our house in Syracuse: a washing machine, a dryer, a dishwasher, an upright refrigerator, and a husband to lean on.

Washing sheets was an arduous task since they were the old-fashioned linen kind that her father was given by his mother when he was married. Yvonne and her mother washed them in the bathtub; and when the sheets were wet, they could hardly lift them to wring them out by hand. Then they had to carry the sheets outside to hang on the clothesline. It was a real workout, but they just laughed and announced they needed a vacation after washday.

Another chore was having to shop for food, since the small refrigerator needed to be replenished often to feed a six-person household. Yvonne had to travel into Turin to purchase some items that the kids ate, like cereal and peanut butter. At that time, this food was not a part of an Italian's diet. Whenever Yvonne went out, the three children were usually brought along. Yvonne's mother, Ines, was a big help in shouldering family tasks; she would mind the children at times, help prepare meals, and assist in getting them to bed. But most importantly, Ines was the adult company Yvonne needed to offset the constant attention she had to give the children.

It wasn't long before many people knew about the denim-dressed "Americana" who spoke Italian, had three small children, and drove her car everywhere. She was an oddity, since most families had no children or at most one child, and at that time not many women in Ivrea drove a car. Italians express enthusiastic warmth when meeting a child, and three little ones really made them overflow with affection. Yvonne felt that the fear of responsibility and the time required to care for a child discourages modern Italian couples from having large families. Also, there was the realization that for many years, huge families caused the migration of millions of Italians to other parts of the world.

A dynamic that made it easier for Yvonne to adapt to her new surroundings was the solicitous attitude many Italian men had toward women. They are definitely considered the weaker sex and need special care. Of course, this thinking can sometimes lead to arrogance, but usually it leads to very friendly and helpful gestures.

Driving around Ivrea with three adults and three children in a little Volkswagen was certainly noticed by the populace. One day especially, while Yvonne was concentrating on finding her way in town, she found herself going the wrong way on a one-way street. An officer approached the car, whipped off his cap, and announced, "Stay calm, Signora, I will help you." She was a woman in distress and he needed to protect her. He then stopped all traffic and gallantly motioned her to make a U-turn and proceed. As Yvonne finished her maneuver, she waved to thank him and he responded by touching the brim of his cap with his index finger. Italians have a very laissez-faire attitude about violating rules.

Another time, Yvonne was driving down a very narrow street when a large truck approached her. As she was carefully driving past the cab of the truck, the driver leaned out and with a wicked smile said, "Cuddle up, Signora, cuddle up." She couldn't help but laugh, and it eased her tension. Being considered a dependent female does have its advantages.

Adding to Yvonne's feeling of being comfortable were the several relatives that were in the area; visits with them were her only diversion from caring for the children. Their stopovers made her and the children feel welcome, especially when Uncle Baldo came over for Sunday dinner. This sixty-one-year-old bachelor built a wonderful relationship with the children by giving them bike rides and playing with them, even though in the beginning they couldn't speak to one another. Through sign language and his desire to please the children, a superb rapport developed. Most Sundays he rode his bicycle about five miles from his village of Vestigne into Ivrea. After dinner and several glasses of wine, Yvonne felt a bike ride home wasn't a good idea, so she crammed Baldo and his bike into her little Volkswagen and drove him home.

No matter where Yvonne went in town, she felt that people knew who she was; she surprised them when she spoke the local dialect. It made her seem like one of them, and as a result, merchants were always pleased to wait on her. Even the money exchanger offered her service that went beyond an Italian's usual helpful attitude. He exchanged Yvonne's American bank dollar checks for lira; and when he periodically went to Switzerland, he cashed them.

It was obvious to everyone she met that Yvonne was an independent young lady, and she became more aware of this fact when she went away for a few days and met a young Italian mother by herself with two small children. Elena couldn't drive, and her husband drove her to the hotel for her respite from housewifely tasks. She was amazed when she realized that Yvonne ran her household in the States with no help from either parents or servants. Sharing with grandparents the raising of children is quite common in Italy, and some say that not wanting to overburden parents is one reason for small families.

Yvonne demonstrated to Elena her independence and grit one day when they went off with the five children to visit some castles. They found themselves on a paved road that supposedly led to a nearby castle, but soon the way turned into a dirt road, and then a narrow one-lane mountain path without barriers. It was time to turn around, but the width of the path made it a difficult undertaking. Elena got out of the car and helped Yvonne negotiate the numerous maneuvers required to get the car pointed down the road. Yvonne is fearful of heights but she was determined not to panic, and with prayers for help to St. Anthony she managed to finally get the car turned around. I am sure Elena was impressed, as I was when I heard about the composure Yvonne showed when so many people depended on her.

Our two oldest children learned about the warmth and hospitality of the Italian nuns and spoke some Italian when they were enrolled in a summer daycare program. Yvonne was amazed how well the little children were able to communicate in spite of the language differences. The nuns were teachers in schools for older children; this assignment was a vacation for them, and they loved spoiling the little ones. Yvonne beamed with pride when she was told how well our two offspring behaved.

Our children were too young to remember much about living in Ivrea, but somehow through our reminding them over the years they all developed an attachment for the place and found opportunities to return. I am proud of Yvonne for having the skill and self-sufficiency to successfully take advantage of the chance to live in a different culture. It was a confidence-builder for her in facing our future together.

A GOOD SAMARITAN

Getting help from a Turkish taxi driver when passing through Istanbul made for an interesting travel experience.

I had been working for four months, twelve hours a day, seven days a week, at a U.S. Air Force site in eastern Turkey. Having little time except for work and sleep made it easier to live in this place where progress seemed centuries behind the rest of the world. I had made a few excursions into the nearby ancient walled town of Diyabikar, built by the Romans, and got a glimpse of life in this primitive part of Turkey. Walking about the town and seeing so many examples of primal existence always made me self-conscious and uncomfortable. I much preferred life at the base, which was an oasis in this very arid and inhospitable land since it had some American culture with its movies, cold beer, and an occasional steak dinner. The work to install radar to track Russian missile launches was exciting and very interesting, but I was ready for a break and a return to the more affluent way of western life. In the field they refer to this as R&R.

Through base personnel I was able to make reservations to fly Turkish Airlines to Istanbul and connect with an Air France flight to Milan, Italy, where my wife would meet me. There was one complication: my flight to Milan left the day after I arrived in Istanbul. For reasons I was never able to understand, I was not able to make a reservation for a room in Istanbul. I was told, "Don't worry. Just go to the Air France office in the city and they will find you lodging." They made it sound so simple.

Simple is how one would describe the facilities at the Diyabikar Airport where I began my trip. It had a small run-down clay terminal building with a single runway. Fortunately, the plane that arrived was modern. We left in midafternoon, but with stops in Malatya and Ankara we didn't arrive until eight in the evening. I hadn't eaten since early that morning. Also, inhaling the smoke on the plane from Turkish cigarettes for the past few hours had made me a little nauseous and uncomfortable, so I was looking forward to getting into a hotel and having something to eat.

The Istanbul terminal was modern, and on my way over I had passed through it on my Pan Am flight before I reached Ankara. I spent two nights in Turkey's capital waiting for my Turkish Airlines flight to Diyabikar. The city was quite modern, in contrast to what I would observe as I went further east. I knew something about Istanbul's storied history and wished I could have spent some time there to see the place. However, my focus now was to find some lodging. Outside the terminal there was an abundance of taxis, but I didn't know how to tell the driver where to take me. I had to do something, so I got into the first cab.

The driver turned to me with a smile on his face and said, "Where do you want to go, sir?" I was at first stunned and then relieved by my good fortune in finding a cabbie who spoke English. His thick mustache was the only thing that seemed to distinguish him from a New York City cab driver.

"Do you know where the Air France office is?"

"Yes, it is not far from the airport." The man spoke with little accent, and I became curious about his background.

"How did you learn to speak English so well?"

"Oh, I have a brother who lives in America. Several years ago I went to live with him for a short while. Being a cab driver, I find English helps me a lot."

I now relaxed and felt a lot better about being in this ancient place. As I took in some of the sights, I could see that the city has a modern appearance along with its mideastern character. I was asked, "How long are you staying?"

"Only one night. I am on my way to meet my wife in Milan, Italy. I was told Air France could find me room for the night."

"I know visitors have difficulty finding a room in Istanbul."

I didn't like what I was hearing. Soon we arrived at a small Air France office on a busy commercial street. When I entered the office, I noticed a number of people crowded around a single clerk who was carrying on several conversations at once. Some were speaking English, so I could tell everyone was trying unsuccessfully to find a place to spend the night. I thought it would be a waste of time to join the crowd at that time. I stepped outside to collect my thoughts and figured one option would be to return to the airport and sleep in a chair.

The look on my face must have alerted the cabbie waiting outside for me that there was a problem. He asked, "What's the matter?" I told him about the chaotic situation inside, and he immediately said, "Don't worry. I know a woman who has a house that rents rooms. I am sure she will have one for you."

I wasn't really sure how to respond to his suggestion. The man seemed friendly and genuine in wanting to help, but I was concerned about accepting his offer. After some hesitation, I tried to give a positive reply. "It sounds like a better idea than sleeping at the airport."

Soon after I got back in the cab, we left the commercial area and went into an especially modest residential neighborhood. I began having second thoughts about my decision. The cabbie appeared to try and reassure me by saying, "We will soon be there." Shortly we pulled in front of a two-story building on a street of rowhouses. I followed the cab driver—who now seemed like a friendly tour guide—up some steps, and after he rang the bell a slender young woman in modern dress came to the door. She was in stark contrast to my earlier close encounters with Turkish women. One was an exotic belly dancer at a Diyabikar restaurant and the other, when stepping out of her apartment house, immediately covered her face with a scarf. You can see why I might have had a rather strange view of Turkish women. Abdul then began explaining to her in Turkish my need for a room. She turned to me and smiled and said in English, "You are most welcome in my house." I noticed that the house was quite dark and the only light came from some candles and an oil lamp. She become aware of my puzzled look and said, "In this part of the city, they turn off the electricity at ten o'clock."

The cab driver looked like he was getting ready to leave. I said to him, "You have been so kind this evening. I don't know what I would have done without you. Could you please tell me what your name is?"

He seemed pleased that I wanted to know and said, "Abdul. If you want, I can pick you up tomorrow and take you to the airport."

"That would be wonderful. My flight is at 10:00 a.m."

"I'll be here at eight o clock."

As he was going out the door, I gave him a generous tip and said, "Thank you again for all your help."

My hostess turned to me and said, "Can I show you to your room?"

A lot of my anxiety now left me and I realized I was quite hungry, so I said, "I haven't eaten since early this morning; is there something you can prepare for me to eat?"

She was surprised by my request, thought for a minute, then said, "How about some scrambled eggs?"

"That would be wonderful." I soon had a plate of eggs and a slice of bread to placate my hunger. My hostess sat down and told me about the problems of losing power. It seems neighborhoods took turns sharing the electricity.

Like Abdul, she spoke English quite well, and I wondered aloud where she had learned the language. She said, "I was taught English in school, and dealing with tourists has helped me not to lose what I learned."

After I finished eating, she found a flashlight and led me to my room. It contained a single bed and a dresser and looked neat and well cared for. The only oddity was that the bed had a sag in the middle, but the sheets were clean and I had no trouble feeling comfortable. Before I fell off to sleep, I wondered if Abdul would return the next morning.

I got up at seven o'clock, washed, got dressed, and waited for Abdul to show. I was offered a cup of coffee, but I wasn't ready for the thick black brew the Turks like. Promptly at eight, Abdul appeared and I again felt thankful for his concern and willingness to be helpful. I paid for my room and food and thanked my hostess for her thoughtfulness. I wasn't really sure exactly why I had received such care and kindness. I know that I saw a side of the Turkish people that my company orientation course had not introduced me to.

On the way to the airport, Abdul asked, "Did you sleep well last night?"

"Yes. The room was quite comfortable, and I really appreciated the eggs she prepared for me. Have you taken many people to her?"

"Not too many. But I knew she would treat you well."

When we reached the airport, I profusely thanked him again and said, "Abdul, you turned the problem I was having into a memorable experience."

He smiled and said, "As a cab driver I get many chances to be helpful, and I am glad you will have a happy memory of your visit to Istanbul."

Soon after entering the airport, I went and made a hotel reservation for my return. I enjoyed the experience I had, but I thought I might not be as lucky next time.

When I returned, I had a room at the fancy Hotel Hilton. However, the accommodations left a little to be desired, since they put me in a poolside cabana. My modest room without any electricity had advantages I hadn't appreciated, but I most valued the people I met and whom I will never forget.

Birthing and Passing

These life occurrences create remembrances that need to be recorded.

The beginning and end of life for family members always leave impressions that are hard to forget. One is an occasion for joy, while the other brings with it the feeling of sorrow. Yet each is often called a celebration. I would say that for me the word aptly describes the former, but celebration is not how I would describe the latter.

The birth of each of our three children had some circumstances that made them a bit different and therefore memorable. When our first child, Susan, was born, we were renting a small apartment in Solvay, a village bordering Syracuse. The owner of the house lived downstairs. She had a daughter, Lorraine, who was about Yvonne's age and already had two children. When Yvonne found out she was pregnant, she spoke to Grace, Lorraine's mother, who suggested that she call her daughter about making arrangements to visit an obstetrician. During their phone conversation, Yvonne discovered that Lorraine was also pregnant and she suggested that they make consecutive appointments to see her doctor. Yvonne couldn't drive at the time, and Lorraine needed someone to watch her two children during her visit. Therefore, the arrangement suited each other's needs, and throughout their pregnancies they arranged to go together to see the doctor. As a result, they became good friends.

When Yvonne's birthing pains started, it was early evening and I was there to comfort her. She calmly waited. Late that night when the interval between contractions reached the rate at which it was time to leave for the hospital, we slowly made our way to the car. I unhurriedly drove to the emergency entrance and then made my way to the waiting room.

As Yvonne was getting comfortable in her room, she heard a familiar voice in the hall. She called out, "Is that you, Lorraine?" Shortly Lorraine poked her head in the door and said hello. Each now having a child born on the same day would increase their friendship.

When Lorraine's husband, Michael, walked into the waiting room, I was both surprised and grateful. Here was a man with fatherhood knowledge and who could make my waiting a better experience. We gabbed for a while, and then the nurse came in and told Michael he was the father of his second son. He hurried off to see the baby and I continued my vigil. Finally, early that morning, I received the news that my daughter Susan was born. Seeing your child and wife after all her hard work is over made me realize that I had missed out on witnessing one of life's miracles—though not observing Yvonne's labor pains was a relief to me!

Susan's birth was straightforward and went along much as we had expected. The births of our two sons were much more complicated.

A little over two years later, Yvonne was getting ready to deliver our second child. In early afternoon of a nice summer day she was talking with our neighbor, Betty, who was going to watch Susan when Yvonne went to the hospital. Suddenly Yvonne received a strong and prolonged pain, and Betty suggested that Yvonne call me to come home. When I came into the house, Betty had already left and Yvonne was experiencing a lot of discomfort. In a short while, she cried out, "My water has broken." Things were not happening as the last time and I was getting a little anxious. We cleaned up the mess and Yvonne changed her clothes. Her pain was now becoming more severe; she called the doctor, and then I helped her to the car.

After we were seated, she grasped my hand and cried out as her pains occurred. I was now becoming concerned that the birth would soon take place. It was rush hour and the roads were crowded as I drove on a major street to downtown Syracuse as fast as I could safely go. I had one hand on the wheel, and the other was tightly squeezed by Yvonne as she cried out in pain. As I got within a few blocks of the hospital, I encountered a long line of traffic being directed by a policeman. There was no traffic coming the other way, so I decided to pass the tie-up and drove past a very surprised cop. I would have welcomed some help from the law. Arriving at the emergency entrance, I got a nurse to put Yvonne into a wheelchair. When they took her away, I knew that she was in safe hands and breathed a sigh of relief.

I parked the car and immediately after I entered the waiting room, the nurse came and told me a healthy Larry had come into the world. I then realized that I had been a lot closer to witnessing the miracle of birth than I cared to be. It had certainly been a hectic afternoon, but Yvonne's suffering was over more quickly and I certainly felt more involved this time in the blessed event.

Eighteen months later, in the middle of winter, Yvonne was pregnant with our third child. When her first pains occurred I was home, and remembering our last experience, I became a little concerned. She remained calm and patiently waited. Finally she felt it might be time to leave for the hospital and called the doctor. It was late at night with little traffic on the road, and as we arrived in front of the hospital, Yvonne became worried that she might not have been quite ready. She wanted to sit in the car and wait. After awhile we decided having a cup of coffee might help us decide what to do. We went into a diner, and Yvonne expressed her embarrassment about the waiting doctor and having to wake up Betty, who was asleep at home. Yvonne's pains and their frequency started to diminish, and she began to believe what she experienced earlier might have been false labor. She became convinced that the birth wasn't going to happen that night and we should go home. We arrived home and told Betty about the evening's events. She told us the doctor had called the house and she told him we had left some time ago. We found out later the doctor felt Yvonne might still show up and he fell asleep waiting at the hospital. You can now understand why some general practitioners give up handling obstetrics.

We went to sleep. In the morning I got up and left for work, but I repeatedly called to find out how Yvonne was feeling. After dinner that evening, Yvonne's pains returned and she felt she was now ready. After calling Betty, off we went to a different hospital, with the partner of the doctor from the previous evening now on duty. Early that morning, he came out and told me we had a second child with outside plumbing; a healthy Ray had made his appearance.

Recalling these events makes me realize how wonderful it can be to bring a child into this world. For each of our children to subsequently have experienced the same number of blessed events has created a special bond in our relationships.

Thinking about the end of life obviously creates a totally different set of impressions and makes you reflect on your own mortality. My mother, Jennie, was the first of the grandparents to pass away. She was a very attractive, sweet woman and a talented dressmaker. She may have missed out on a lot of what life can offer; she never traveled or took vacations. My mother was hardworking and was both a significant financial contributor to the family and a wonderful caregiver. At the age of fifty, when most people are entering their most productive and often rewarding years, she developed a brain tumor. At the time I was thousands of miles away serving in the army, and I missed out on being able to offer any comfort. Fortunately her operation was a success, but she was not the same energetic woman after.

Several months later, when I returned for my wedding, Mother had almost returned to her former self. I remember how much she enjoyed that day, welcoming her first daughter-in-law into the family. Later, when I was discharged from the army, we spent several months living with my parents, and Yvonne and she became quite close. Families living together for a short time in later years do tend to create bonds that may not have existed earlier. After we left my parents' home and settled in Syracuse, I managed to get them to visit us only once. It was the first time my mother had been away from the city since her honeymoon.

Years later, as I was finishing up a long-term assignment working in Turkey, I received a telegram asking me to come home because my mother was gravely ill. When I returned, I found my mother at home being cared for by my father. She had cancer of the stomach, and the prognosis was not good. My father hired an older woman to stay with Mother while he went to work. He described her as an angel for the comfort and caring support she gave my mother during the six months she suffered before passing away.

I remember feeling at the memorial service that my mother was somewhat shortchanged in life. She had a serious illness at fifty, followed by reduced capabilities and then a long painful period before dying at the age of fifty-nine. Sometime later I realized that her wants had been quite simple and her fulfillment needs were undemanding. Besides, she had a lot to be pleased about. My mother had three children who loved her, ten grandchildren to be proud of, and a husband who stood faithfully by.

After his wife passed away, my father, Charlie, went to live with his sister and brother-in-law in the Bronx. He managed a few times to come and see us in Syracuse, and when we visited Yvonne's mother in Astoria, he was always invited for Sunday dinner. Each time he brought with him the Italian pastries that he loved.

My father was overweight and smoked but appeared to be in good health, although he seldom saw a doctor. Six years after becoming a widower, my father surprised all of his family by announcing he was going to get married. We had heard nothing about him seeing anyone; he was obviously sensitive to what our reaction might be. My siblings and I were happy that he had found someone to share his life with.

Since I was his oldest son, he asked me to accompany his bride down the church aisle and give her away. She was several years younger than my father and had never been married before. The constant smile on her face showed how happy she was to be marrying my father. All the grandchildren especially enjoyed the wedding reception as they got giddy on little sips of whiskey sours they sampled.

The newlyweds left on a three-day honeymoon trip. The day after they returned, I received a call at work from my brother that my father had suffered a heart attack. A day later he died. During the following week, I escorted the teary-eyed widow down the same church aisle that we had traveled just over a week before. The occasion seemed so bizarre, but it showed the unexpected and unusual ways life events can occur.

We never got to know our stepmother very well. She sent our children some gifts that first Christmas after my father passed away, but she turned down our requests to come visit. My brother and sister got the same off-putting reaction, so she faded from our lives. It was unfortunate but understandable, considering what an upsetting experience she had been through.

My father-in-law, Lorenzo, was a timid and hardworking man who made a living as a waiter, serving both lunch and dinner in downtown New York City. He usually came home to Astoria between each meal to see his daughter. He had few outside interests, but enjoyed visits with friends who had links to the Piedmont region of Italy, where he was born and spent his early years. After he retired, his wife, Ines, modernized her mother's home in the small village of Vestigue, and they spent warm months of the year renewing their ties with the old country.

Lorenzo avoided seeing doctors, and his health was marred for years by the ills associated with emphysema. He never stopped smoking in spite of his difficulty breathing until, at the age of seventy-seven, he was admitted to a hospital in Italy; after ten days he passed away. Ines immediately called Yvonne, and in one day she was at her mother's side. In Italy, where embalming is seldom used, wakes are of short duration. In spite of what often seemed like less than a harmonious relationship, Ines was upset by her husband dying and wanted and needed the support that Yvonne gave her. After three weeks of consoling her mother, Yvonne returned to Syracuse. The following year, Ines left her apartment in Astoria and came to live with us in Syracuse when she wasn't at her home in Italy.

Ines lived to the ripe old age of ninety-eight, and I wrote about her life in a separate chapter in this book.

Passing of loved ones is a sorrowful occasion, but something we all face, and remembering their lives is a way of celebrating the event.

Skiing: A Wonderful Lifetime Activity

Years of skiing experiences that my wife and I have enjoyed with our family and friends make for wonderful memories.

Living in Syracuse one has to learn to cope with the large amounts of snow that blanket the area every year. Located south and east of Lake Ontario, the area receives a number of lake effect storms, and an occasional northeaster also contributes to its annual average of over a hundred inches of snow. We dealt with it by shoveling our driveway and saying it was good exercise, getting snow tires and driving carefully, and making sure our cupboard was kept full. It really didn't take long to get used to the winters. Our young children enjoyed the season by sliding down the hill in our backyard. In fact, we gave our grown-up friends sliding parties, where going downhill on a saucer and climbing back up again, combined with a hot toddy and snacks, made for an invigorating and fun evening.

We moved away from the house on the hill and into a new four-bedroom place just blocks away. We were greeted that winter by a storm that occurs very rarely—thirty-eight inches of snow that fell over two days. Most places of work were closed, and staying home to dig out and seeing all the neighbors doing the same thing made the occasion a fun adventure in surviving. The only damage was to businesses that lost money when their workers stayed home.

However, the storm convinced my wife Yvonne and me that we should do more in adapting to the winters and taking advantage of God's gift of snow. Just before Christmas we took ourselves and Ray (age five), Larry (age seven), and Susan (age nine) to a nearby sports store to outfit us all for the ski slopes.

The owner was surprised by the whole family coming to begin skiing at the same time, and we were somewhat amazed ourselves by our venturesome attitude in embracing something we knew nothing about.

During Christmas week we went off to Greek Peak Mountain, the only ski area that was open, and enrolled everyone in lessons. We all went off to the bunny slope and managed to master the rope tow that brought us to the top of a small hill that to beginners appeared daunting. Yvonne and I managed the descent without falling, and our instructor encouraged us enough that we were willing to try again. It was soon apparent that the children were more adept at the sport than Yvonne and I, and their instructor took them to a little more challenging slope. At the end of the day, we were all pleased by our first skiing experience, and we returned the next day for another lesson.

By the end of Christmas week, enough snow had fallen to allow all the ski slopes in the area to open. We went off without an instructor to try out our newfound skill. After trying the easy slopes at several places, we settled on Labrador Mountain as a location that suited us. Once we advanced beyond the bunny slopes and their rope tows, we had to master another skill. At that time most areas used T-bars to get you up to the top of their mountains. The T-bar is a device that is attached to a cable and consists of a fixed cylinder that contains a movable spring-loaded cylinder. At the end of this latter piece is a bar on which you lean your behind. If two people of comparable height go up together, they are fairly easy devices to handle. However, when a child and grown-up go together, the bar rests on the child's behind, but with the adults it rests somewhere along their thighs, making the device somewhat unstable. Yvonne found that going up with Ray made her very nervous and unsure of herself, and she would at times lose her balance and fall off the tow. This is somewhat of an embarrassing experience. For me it presented even more of a problem, so most times Yvonne got stuck going up with Ray. Fortunately, it didn't take long for Ray to master going up the T-bar by himself.

Skiing is not an easy sport to learn. It requires proper technique, along with good balance and no fear about falling. However, it is an individual activity since you decide the steepness of the slope you go down and the speed at which you wish to travel. You usually descend the hill faster than you go up, so it's nice to have company on the lift. Only during the first year did the children ski with Yvonne and me; their greater skill and boldness made them patiently wait for us at the bottom as we slowly made our way down.

When the children were young, skiing required more effort on our part than just going up and down a hill. There was all the clothing to be gathered and put on the children, loading all the boots and skis into the car, and preparing lunches for five people. It was sometimes an exhausting day, but always a rewarding one. I constantly noticed on the drive home each child falling asleep and looking so content from his invigorating day of skiing. When we arrived home, their appetites showed the energy they needed to replenish. At the end of our first season of skiing, we all agreed that the activity had been a resounding success.

We started the next season by attending a Warren Miller movie. Each year Mr. Miller produces a film extolling the joys and fun of skiing. He makes you laugh and renews your desire to get back on the slopes. Afterward, I went out and bought a season pass for the whole family at Labrador Mountain. By February of that year, we felt we were accomplished enough skiers to head off to the bigger mountains of Vermont.

It was an exhilarating time the day we went to Mt. Snow, but the most excitement occurred on our first ride up the lift. I was escorting Ray on the lift line, which contained a wooden barrier to guide skiers as they approached the chairlift. Ray and I had little experience with this type lift, and my attention was focused on making sure Ray was prepared for the chair. I wasn't watching my skis, and when the chair picked us up, my skis were pushed into the barrier alongside the chair. We were both safely seated, but I had one ski release from my boot and it was dangling from the safety strap. My son thought this was funny and started laughing, but I was in a bit of a panic because we were approaching a midstation where the chair clears the dismounting slope by only a couple of feet. I hastily grabbed my ski and held it against my boot as we went past the midstation. My antics made Ray's laughing grow louder, but I ignored him because my next problem was getting off the lift at the top. Skiing on one ski with another one dragging next to you presents problems an amateur wants to avoid. As we approached the getting-off point, I yelled to the lift operator, who saw my plight and stopped the lift. He gradually moved the lift until I could put my ski down on the snow. I stumbled and slid down the slope far enough so the chair would pass over me. Ray stopped laughing long enough to help me up, and I was able to again attach my ski to the boot. The experience was the first of many uncomfortable situations on the slopes, but they never discouraged my enthusiasm for the sport. I was so convinced that skiing was good for our family that the next year I bought a thousand-dollar bond to help finance development at Labrador Mountain. It was a great investment since it gave you 7 percent interest and an adult membership for free. I was earning 17 percent on my investment, and for over twenty years I saw no reason to redeem the bond.

Over the years our children became very good skiers and were asked to join the Labrador ski team, but we discouraged it. They were already involved in so many competitive activities at school that we felt skiing should be done just for the fun it provided. Fortunately they all agreed with our thinking. Each year we managed to take the children skiing at some of the bigger mountains in New York state and Vermont. Particularly enjoyable were the years we spent going to the Onondaga Ski Club Lodge in Vermont with our neighbors, the Bertzes. They had five children, and with our three we took up a lot of space at the rustic lodge. We brought food to feed everyone for breakfast and dinner, and mealtime was a big family affair. On the slopes the children split up into groups, but we could always count on them to come in and have lunch with us parents. Our families became very close since the Bertzes also skied at Labrador and lived across the street from us. As everyone grew older, the friendships continued to be maintained.

When the children were twelve, fourteen, and sixteen, we took them on a trip to Europe. I was able to combine work activities with vacation time to let us spend six weeks enjoying the charm of many overseas cultures. One of the things we planned on trying to do was skiing the glaciers of Cervinia in July. We packed some warm clothes and planned to rent the other things we needed. We made arrangements to stay at a small comfortable hotel owned by a friend of Yvonne's from her youth, Leonardo Carrel, who was also a ski instructor, mountain-climbing guide, and a wonderful host. After arriving, we immediately went to rent our skiing equipment for our two-day stay. Afterward, the children were playing around the hotel when Larry had a freakish accident and slammed his hand into a stone step and broke the middle finger of his right hand. Leonardo sent us to see a doctor friend of his who was staying at the hotel. He said he could easily make a splint for the finger, but he needed to buy the necessary material the following day. The disappointed look on Larry's face told the doctor that he anticipated not being able to ski. The next words out of the doctor's mouth made Larry smile. He said, "You can ski; just pack some snow around your finger whenever you can to keep it from swelling too much."

Larry had no trouble following the doctor's orders and also enjoying skiing with all of us down gentle slopes, in brilliant sunshine, surrounded by majestic mountain peaks. At noon the snow became too soft, and it was time to return to our hotel for a nice Italian lunch. After eating a big portion of polenta ciocciara, which consists of thick slices of polenta layered with a mushroom tomato sauce and a tasty mountain cheese called fontina, everyone was ready for an afternoon siesta. I still recall our sunburned children sprawled out asleep in chaises on the hotel patio, soaking up the sun with the most contented looks on their faces.

That evening the doctor attended to Larry's finger, and for the next several weeks Larry walked around showing off his finger splint by raising it in the air; I was always concerned people would get offended by his gesture. We tried to pay the doctor, but he would let us treat him only to a glass of wine.

That evening the children retired early, and Leonardo invited Yvonne and me to join him and a couple of friends in sharing a friendship drink. It is a mountain tradition: warm seasoned wine is put into a large wooden bowl with a cover with six drinking spouts carved around the edge, making it easy for everyone to share the drink. Leonardo took a sip and turned the bowl so Yvonne could drink from the next spout. After several trips around the bowl, you begin to forget and not care which spout is yours. As the bowl continues to get refilled, you begin to feel that you have known your companions all your life. Even understanding only a little of the conversation taking place, I had a strong feeling of good fellowship.

The next day was a repeat of our wonderful skiing experience of the previous day, and after another hearty lunch and a short siesta we left. During the drive down the mountain and through the Aosta Valley, the car was filled with excited talk reliving the ski trip we would always remember.

Once our children went to college, their days of skiing were limited to the time when they returned at Christmas; and after college, except for Larry, their days on the slopes became rare. Larry met some friends who belonged to the Onondaga Ski Club, and he managed to continue to spend some time each winter skiing.

When our children no longer skied with Yvonne and me, our interest in the sport did not diminish. We continued our membership in the ski club and spent weekends at Labrador, and each year we signed up for the club's trips to ski out west. We skied at many well-known places like Aspen, Vail, Breckenridge, Copper, and Jackson Hole. The abundant sun, good snow, and long runs increased our appreciation for skiing, and the trips were the highlight of our winter.

I remember on our first trip out west to Aspen, we had a nice lunch with some wine. At 8000 feet, the wine's effect is much more potent, and Yvonne became excited about her skiing ability. Outside the restaurant was a run named the Wall, and she wanted to try going down it. I took a look and decided her judgment was under the influence and talked her out of being a daredevil.

Visiting the famous resorts out west is not just about enjoying a ski adventure, but also involves getting to know other club members traveling with you. Relaxing in a hot tub, soothing your tired muscles and talking over your daily experiences, is a great way to get to know people. Sharing a meal with friends with a hearty appetite at the numerous fine restaurants is a wonderful way to end the day. Sleeping is never a problem.

Another time at Aspen, wine may have contributed to my only serious skiing mishap. It was a beautiful warm sunny day, when a ski cap and jacket were unnecessary. After a nice lunch on the mountain enhanced by a glass of wine, I decided I wanted to continue my descent by going down a groomed expert trail. Yvonne said she would meet me at the bottom of the run, so off I went and after a few turns I lost my balance and went tumbling down. Both skis released and accompanied me down the hill—this was before skis had safety brakes. When I finally stopped falling, one of my skis hit my bare head before coming to rest. I was a little stunned and felt blood as I just lay there. Two skiers came to see if I needed help. Seeing my cut, one skier said he would go off to find the ski patrol while the other stayed behind to comfort me. From down below, Yvonne saw what happened and wondered what she could do. Soon two burly guys with a toboggan came to my aid. They gave me gauze to absorb the blood, tucked me into the toboggan, and off we went. On the way down, the ski patrol stopped by Yvonne and told her to follow them.

I soon began to enjoy my newfound way down a mountain. My rescuers introduced themselves and were polite and friendly. At the base of the mountain, they introduced Yvonne and me to two equally gracious ambulance attendants. At the hospital a very pleasant doctor introduced himself and put nine stitches in my scalp. Yvonne whispered to me, "I wonder when they will serve us tea and cookies." The charming treatment ended when the nurse pointed to the bus stop where I could get a ride back to our condominium. Fortunately, I was back on the slopes the next day and lost only an afternoon of skiing.

During our early days skiing out west, the club packed a lot of activity into a week. For example, one time we flew out of Syracuse early Friday evening; after arriving in Denver, we went by bus to a small hotel about an hour from Aspen, checking in at about two in the morning. After a late breakfast we dressed in our ski apparel and were driven to the Aspen Highlands ski area for a half-day of skiing while our luggage was delivered to our condo. For the next seven days we skied at one of the four areas near Aspen. On Sunday, a day of rest for some people, we headed for the airport, but on the way we made a stop at Copper Mountain for a day of skiing. We took a red-eye to Syracuse, arriving at six in the morning. I was late for work and left early. After that experience, we made sure our future trips were more relaxing.

Vail is arguably the mecca of ski areas. It's huge, with several vast bowls on the back side of the mountain, while numerous trails and lifts fill the other side. I had progressed in my skiing ability to where I advertised that I could ski any groomed trail, and many expert trails received such treatment. My son Larry was with us on the trip, and in his travels around the mountain he found a double black diamond trail that had been groomed and asked if I was interested in trying it. My boast was being challenged, so I had to accept the invitation. When I came to the top of the trail, I wondered what equipment they used to groom such a steep ski run; falling would certainly result in a long body slide and some difficulty in reattaching my skis. However, I was determined to try it. I started off slowly and cautiously; with each turn my confidence grew, and when I reached the bottom I was real proud of myself. I believe my son was also impressed.

Yvonne has always been an enthusiastic skier in spite of suffering from a fear of heights. Most of us have some uneasiness with heights, but in Yvonne's case it is a more acute sensation. She didn't experience it skiing until she went out to the big mountains out west. At times on these mountains, she gets a view of their vastness, which increases her nervousness. In a cable car she will always look up the mountain; and when skiing a narrow ridge, she feels drawn to the edge and needs to focus her attention straight ahead. In spite of these moments of discomfort, she has always managed to control her fears and enjoy the sport. However, on one occasion she needed some help.

We were skiing at Jackson Hole, which consists of two mountains, one for intermediate and novice skiers and another for experts, although there are some less challenging ways to get down this latter mountain. After two days of skiing the less difficult area, Yvonne and I decided to go with our son Larry and some friends up the more demanding mountain. When we got off the lift, I knew Yvonne would have problems. We were on the narrow peak of the mountain surrounded by nothing but blue sky; it was like being on top of the world. Yvonne nervously skied over to the edge of the peak, where her eyes got to see a huge bowl and her legs turned to jelly. My son could see his mother's plight and tried to reassure her. He said, "I will ski in front of you, and if you only look at my back we will get down." Bolstered by Larry's confidence, they started off. I followed and I could see Yvonne intensely following Larry's instructions, and soon her nervousness abated as she reached the bottom. The smile on her face showed she was proud of her accomplishment. However, we did not return to try that run again.

During the years I skied out west, I also had the opportunity to ski in Italy. I had arranged to spend the weekends before and after a business project in Milan visiting with Yvonne's cousin Franco and his wife, Ines. They lived about an hour away by train in the small town of Robbio. On Sunday, they thought instead of struggling with our lack of skills in each other's language, that a trip to a nearby ski area would be a more pleasant experience for me.

On the way up in the cable car, Ines spoke to two English-speaking Italians about guiding me around the mountain. Franco and Ines were going to spend their time waiting for me in a restaurant on the hill. My guides led me through a boulder-strewn field of snow to a narrow trail that wound its way down between the tips of huge evergreens on one side and the rocky face of the mountain on the other side. My companions warned me about slowing down for a sharp turn ahead, where a net was installed to catch any careless skier. Fearing for my life, I broke into a cold sweat and my legs became quite unsteady. On reaching the bottom, my guides asked if I wanted to make another run, but I politely refused and said I had to meet Franco and Ines for lunch.

After eating, my courage returned and I decided to try the slopes above the restaurant. After getting off the lift, I noticed the weather was getting worse; I was becoming eager to get off the mountain. Near the bottom of the slope, I fell and both bindings released. I struggled for a while getting them attached, and when I looked up, the weather had become extremely bad. The snow and clouds had made the visibility nonexistent; I could hear voices but could see no one. People's voices guided me to the safety of the restaurant, where Ines and Franco awaited me. Not being able to communicate my frustration to them, I smiled and told them I was ready to leave. They seemed to understand; maybe the sweat on my face gave me away. The day gave me a ski experience I could never forget.

The following weekend I was taken to Cervinia and the Hotel Carrel— and another meeting with Leonardo Carrel, who was a longtime friend of Franco and Ines. The Cervinia ski area is vast, and no matter where you go, the Matterhorn (Cervino in Italian) appears to be close by. If you are in the mood for a culture change, you can ski a trail that heads for Switzerland; and after skiing seven miles, you will be in Zermatt.

Leonardo spent the afternoon skiing with me, and my confidence and style greatly improved from the previous weekend. The next day the weather was perfect: blue skies, mild temperatures, and good snow. On my first trip to the top, I became friendly with a group of Englishmen on a holiday, and they invited me to ski with them. They were a fun-loving bunch, and we skied all over that immense mountain, including part of the Swiss Alps. I had a ball and skied until I was exhausted. When I returned, Franco and Ines were worried and concerned because I had not returned for lunch. They thought there must be something seriously wrong when an Italian skips his noonday meal.

In the span of one week, I had gone through the extreme opposite of skiing experiences and I was impressed with how flexible you had to be in coping with the conditions you encounter. Although I have had several moments when I felt uncomfortable skiing, I soon forget them and look forward to my next run down the mountain.

Several years later I returned with Yvonne to ski in Italy. We planned to celebrate our twenty-fifth wedding anniversary by first skiing in the mountains of Piedmont near where Yvonne's mother had her home and then joining a sightseeing tour of Spain and Portugal. During our ten days in Italy, we traveled to Sestriere, due west of Turin, and Cervinia, Courmayeur, and Pila, in the Valle d'Aosta; all areas are about an hour and a half from Yvonne's mother Ines's house in Vestigue. Our strategy, except for Pila, was to arrive in time for a nice Italian lunch and to look over the town. We would then get a good night's sleep so we could get up early and hit the slopes. After skiing all day, we would return to Ines's house for a late supper. We made going to Pila a single-day trip since it was much closer.

At Cervinia, we skied on a beautiful sunny day, and having been there before, I wished to explore more of the mountain. There was a trail off the east end of the Plateau Rosa that would take you down to the base, a run of about six miles, or if you really wanted to travel, you could take an intersecting trail that led to Valtournache several miles farther down the valley. It wasn't a steep trail, but as Yvonne and I started down, I realized we were the only ones skiing on it. I have a picture I took looking down on this area from the plateau and it is an awesome sight of snow and mountain peaks, but it was an eerie and scary feeling to be alone in the middle of the vast snowfield that surrounded us. We had no choice but to continue down, and then we encountered a marker that said the trail was closed farther on because it had not been groomed. We were directed to another trail that soon led to a populated area of skiers, and we were relieved.

For our last run of the day, we went back to the top of Plateau Rosa. Standing in brilliant sunshine, we looked down the mountain, and about 1,500 feet below was this large white cloud. We could not avoid it, and we wondered what it would be like to ski through it. When we entered the cloud, we were engulfed in a very weird effect. The light from above gave a yellow glow to all the water particles in the cloud, but the mist that was created was so dense that our visibility was severely limited. We could hear the grooming machines beginning their descent down the mountain, but we could not see them. We proceeded cautiously until we arrived at the cable car station and felt that prudence was advised, so we decided to ride down. After descending several hundred feet, we broke out of the cloud and were treated to a wonderful view of the valley. At the time we would have preferred to see it from our skis.

Getting to Pila, the closest of the ski resorts, required us to drive for about twenty-five minutes up a narrow, winding road out of Aosta. It was snowing a little at the time, and as I was slowly negotiating a sharp turn, I came upon a snowplow going the other way. We could not pass each other unless one of us backed up. Since he was bigger, I thought it wise if I volunteered. If you think driving on a mountain road in forward gear is intimidating, try it in reverse. After going a short distance, I found a spot where the shoulder widened, and I snuggled up to the guardrail. The snowplow driver gave me a wave and a smile as he passed, but I was too tense to return the greeting.

The skiing at Pila was similar to areas in the United States because many of the trails were cut through the trees. We had decided to ski one area that was accessible only by a long Poma lift. For those who are not skiers, a Poma lift consists of a small saucer-shaped plate that is attached to a short bar that is, in turn, connected to a rope attached to the cable that takes you to the top. You place the bar between your legs, rest your fanny on the saucer, and away you go. We don't have too many in the States, but they were fairly popular in Europe. This particular one was quite fast and pulled you up some very steep grades that went through some wooded areas.

As I rode up, I thought it would be quite easy to fall off since the track we traveled was hardpacked and icy in some places. About halfway up I heard Yvonne cry out that she had fallen off. She was in a section where the skiing trail was accessible, but I was in an area where the woods blocked the path, so I decided to go to the top. I wasn't sure what Yvonne would do, so I decided to wait at the top for a while. When she didn't come, I thought she was waiting at the bottom for me. So down I went, but there was no Yvonne. The only answer could be that she went up the lift and was waiting on top for me.

Another trip up was beginning to cause me some concern, along with a lot of frustration. When I got off the lift, there was no Yvonne to be found. I didn't know whether to get back on the merry-go-round or stay. Since I was getting tired, the decision was easy. As I was waiting, a skier in a ski patrol uniform approached me and asked in heavily accented English, "Have you lost a wife?" I answered yes and then I asked, "Have you found her?" He then explained that Yvonne had talked to him about our problem and he volunteered to come looking for me. She described my very bright yellow and blue ski outfit, which would make me easy to spot. I raced down the hill and there she was. We both had embarrassed looks on our faces and felt that our escapades were like an old-fashioned comedy.

Courmayeur is considered the most popular ski resort in the Valle d'Aosta. It tries hard to replicate the ambiance of an alpine village, but somehow there is something lacking. Again, like at Cervinia, the skiing is not too challenging. However, the vistas are magnificent, the sun was shining, and the snow was good. What more could one ask for?

Mussolini conceived Sestriere as Italy's dream ski resort, but many view the mountain as being rather bleak and the resort is considered somewhat bland. We also learned because of what happened to us that skiing is not the top priority at Sestriere. We had spent the morning under cloudy skies, and then the noonday sun broke through and we looked forward to skiing under bright and warm conditions. When we completed a run, we noticed the lift had stopped and the other lifts we could observe were also not running. We thought they had lost power on the mountain, and we returned to the base lodge, where Yvonne found out the lifts were stopped because it was now lunchtime. It tells you something about Italian priorities. At two o'clock, the mountain returned to life. With our energies restored, we were able to ski until the last lift closed.

As you might have guessed from some of my comments, I was less than impressed by the Italian ski areas. I have a similar feeling about some of the places in Austria and Germany where I have skied. Compared to the ski resorts out west, they are not nearly as interesting. However, the après-ski ambiance often has a charm you don't find at home.

In early 1988 I was appointed to be the technical director of a consortium that General Electric had joined with three other companies. It was an exciting opportunity, and for the next four years Yvonne and I lived in Munich to carry out my assignment. The city is near the alpine ski areas of Austria and northeast Italy, so we brought with us from home our downhill and cross-country skis. Unfortunately, during our time in Germany, we spent less time than we anticipated skiing. The weather often didn't cooperate, and since many of the mountains are not at a really high altitude, conditions were often not appealing. We spent almost as much time cross-country skiing with our friends, the Fermes, as going downhill skiing. In Munich in the winter, snow would remain on the ground for about two weeks and skiing in the English Gardens became a lot of fun. During these times I remember seeing some people getting about by skiing while others were riding their bikes.

Skiing in Austria was quite different. You had to protect your position in the lift line from very aggressive and pushy skiers. Many of the lifts covering the wide range of areas throughout the central Austria Alps were run and maintained by different towns in the valley, and it was wise to buy a pass that covered adjoining areas. You might find yourself unable to get back up after a run if you went outside the town's control. Since the lift complex was under different ownerships, I believe it may have slowed down incorporating the modern equipment we saw out west.

While we lived in Munich we experienced two memorable skiing excursions. On one occasion late in the season, skiing was only possible on the upper part of the mountain, and you had to go up two lifts before you could reach the area where there was snow. After enjoying our day on the mountain it was time to return, but we overlooked one thing. Getting back to our car required riding down the first lift we had come up. When Yvonne realized that she would now have to look from a great height down the steep slope, panic set in. I tried to explain we had no choice, but in her mind there was always the option of walking down. I said this wasn't practical. Finally the lift operator came to our rescue. He told her to give him her skis and to close her eyes, and he led her off to the stopped chairlift. She sat down and he put her skis in the basket beside her and off we went. All the way down Yvonne never opened her eyes until I told her we had reached the bottom of the slope. Fortunately, she never thought about her predicament until we were leaving, so she was able to ski all day without a concern.

At another time we went on a ski vacation in February with our friends the Robbs. We traveled to a mountain called Kronplatz just across the Austrian border into Italy. It is a rather unexciting place that extols the fact that their skiing terrain has 80 percent beginner slopes and 20 percent intermediate skiing opportunities. Obviously, anyone looking for a little challenge should go someplace else. One problem with easy ski runs is that beginners will often gather more speed than they can handle, and one such skier upset our ski vacation.

Yvonne and I were standing by the ski rack, preparing to store our skis before going in for lunch. An out-of-control German skier came crashing into us, knocking both of us to the ground. I was thrown to one side, while Yvonne fell on her back. She was afraid to move, and while she lay there Maureen Robb, who spoke German, gave the reckless skier a tongue-lashing and threatened him with a lawsuit. The ski patrol arrived and helped Yvonne into the restaurant; after making her comfortable, they sent for an Italian carabiniere to resolve the accident. After awhile a very good-looking Italian policeman came to where we were sitting and started asking questions. He told us if we were serious about suing, Yvonne should go to a hospital and be examined. Somehow the passing of time and the carabiniere's polite expressions of concern and comfort were making Yvonne feel better. She was soon able to walk to the nearby lift, and we all returned to the hotel together. The next day Yvonne still hurt and was in no condition to ski, so the Robbs and I returned to the mountain while she rested at the hotel.

Unfortunately, our ski holiday was suffering another setback. The weather had become very warm and late spring conditions were setting in, and the only challenging slope was crowded with skiers. The Robbs and I decided that going back to keep Yvonne company was a better use of our time. It turned out that though Yvonne's back still hurt, she could walk without discomfort, so we all set out on a hike that stimulated our appetite for the generous delicious evening meal. We never returned to the slopes and spent the remainder of the week exploring the surrounding area on foot. Skiing was obviously a disappointment, but being able to share the balmy weather with good friends still made our vacation very enjoyable. We never pursued a suit, but hoped our irresponsible skier learned a lesson.

I returned to Syracuse shortly after my sixty-second birthday, and within five months I retired from General Electric. After four exciting years working in Europe, I thought it was a good way to end my professional career. While trying to plan my life after work, I thought back to a conversation I had years before while riding up the ski lift at Jackson Hole. My companion was a retired California state trooper, and he was regaling me with the pleasures of living in a ski town; I remember envying him. I now thought that living like a ski bum for a little while would be a fantastic retirement activity, and Yvonne agreed with me.

We picked the northern section of Lake Tahoe as the place to live our fantasy, because we knew people in Truckee who could help us rent a house for the month of March. Arriving in Truckee, which is about 5800 feet above Reno, Nevada, and a couple thousand feet below the Donner Pass summit, with Yvonne and her mother Ines was an eye-opener. None of us had ever seen such an accumulation of snowbanks as filled the streets of this town of 16,000 residences and blocked your view of almost all the places of business. I remember looking for the post office, and although I was in front of it, I never knew it was there. This small town has California's major expressway, Route 80, which goes over the Donner Pass, running through it. The downtown has many good restaurants and little interesting shops, and it's surrounded by communities of very large well-to-do homes. The first house we rented was a comfortable place just outside of the town center, with a nice view of Donner Lake.

Our location was a skier's paradise, with over ten large ski resorts within a short drive and few narrow winding roads to traverse. The biggest resort is Squaw Valley, which was the host for the 1960 Winter Olympics. A little farther south is Aspen Meadows, whose long high-speed chair connects you with some long runs. However, our favorite was Northstar, because it has eight lengthy expert slopes on the back of the mountain, many of which are nicely groomed. These mile-long runs test your ability, and you never want to stop going down, in spite of your aching thighs. However, in the three successive years we skied at Lake Tahoe, we eventually tried all the areas on the north end of the lake and found they all offered ample opportunity to enjoy the sport.

Our life in Truckee was filled with shopping, eating out, meeting our friends, sightseeing, and skiing. At times we felt like natives. We avoided the slopes on the weekends, when the crowds came from the balmy areas down below to our snow community. During the month of March, the weather is not particularly cold, days are longer, the ski base is at its peak, and the skies are usually sunny, so skiing is so very pleasant. We enjoyed taking our numerous guests on car rides around the lake and into the valley towns below. The one thing we didn't do was stop and gamble in the Nevada casinos. We still remember so many delightful experiences from our time spent living and skiing in this very special part of California.

Every year our neighbors, Les and Shirley Bertz, came out to spend time with their sons Scott and Todd. Todd was married, and both Scott and Todd lived in Truckee. Their sons helped us find places to rent and adapt to life at Lake Tahoe. Shirley doesn't downhill ski but she would venture on to a cross-country trail, so sometimes Yvonne and I would find ourselves on those long skis without edges. I often found the way to stop when using them was to just fall down. I preferred going uphill because it was such good exercise. Les has shared many moments skiing with us; for several years he ran a ski trip out west for the ski club, and we often joined his group. While in Truckee, Yvonne and I not only spent time on the slopes with the Bertz family, but we also enjoyed many après-ski moments with them. There were large family dinners at our house or Todd's home. Once Larry, our son, grilled some ribs for over ten of us; and on other occasions we would all go out to dinner together. Scott worked tending bar at Squaw Valley, where we enjoyed him treating us to a beer or hot chocolate before we left the slopes. It was like having family in town.

During our first year in Truckee, the highlight of our stay occurred when Larry, his wife Blair, and their eleven-month-old daughter, Monica, came to spend a week with us. It was a time of family bonding; Ines prepared some meals, we had long cocktail hours, and Monica, who just started walking, danced for us in front of the TV. Besides spending several days together on the slopes, we all went visiting other towns bordering Lake Tahoe. When we went skiing, we took Monica with us; Yvonne and Blair took turns watching her. It was such a pleasure to enjoy our joint fondness for skiing. Larry and Blair showed their mutual love for sharing the sport with us by returning each year we went to California.

During our second year we rented an A-frame house that was several hundred feet above Truckee. It was a newer home, but was lacking in furnishings and amenities. Besides Larry and family, we received a visit from our good friends the Dohertys. It is always more enjoyable skiing with other people. During our third year, we went farther up the area above Truckee. In fact, our house was at the base of the Tahoe Donner Ski Bowl area. It was a big house and great for all the guests we welcomed. Larry and Blair now had another daughter, Ella, with them when they came. Our skiing buddies from Europe, the Robbs, stayed with us for a week; and our son Ray's wife, Tia, and her mother, Shirley, also joined us for a few days. Shirley had never been on skis before, and I admired her tenacity in taking ski lessons and going down the beginner's slopes. However, I believe that she never returned to the slopes after leaving us.

I remember having so many pleasurable moments skiing, but the details of these times fade from your memory bank, while those occasions when conditions tested you are recalled in all aspects. There are two incidents when we encountered this type of experience.

One night we literally had a heavy snowfall: it snowed eighteen inches of what the locals call "Sierra cement." If it isn't packed down, it becomes very difficult to ski on it. The next day I was skiing with a group including Larry,

Blair, and two of Larry's friends at Squaw Valley when someone suggested we ride the Exhibition Chair, which serves an expert area. I was ready to back out but Larry's friend Spencer told me they always groom one trail, so don't worry. After getting off the lift, we all skied down the ridge at the top of the trails looking for the slope that was groomed. The ridge ended, and no packed trail was encountered. Blair, Larry's other friend Johnny, and I were becoming concerned.

The way to ski in heavy snow conditions is to make a shallow traverse of the hill and then jump out of your track and start a new traverse in the opposite direction. Never having skied in these conditions, I was not familiar with the technique—and at my age I was not ready to learn. Johnny was the first to attack the slope. Although not a strong skier, his muscled frame and youth allowed him to survive. Later he started smoking again to soothe his nerves. Blair tried her skill and was having great difficulty and yelled for Larry to help her, but Larry was occupied helping me. She proceeded to make very gentle traverses, and riding a little higher in the snow, she was able to turn and make her way down the hill.

Larry instructed me to traverse the hill, and when I arrived at the edge of the trail, to fall into the uphill side of the mountain. He would come and turn my skis in the opposite direction, and I would initiate another traverse. After several such embarrassing turns, I reached terrain where I could manage by myself. I arrived at the bottom of the hill in a cold sweat from physical exertion and nervous tension. It took awhile before I spoke to Larry's friend Spencer who had told me there was a groomed trail on that hill.

Living in Syracuse, New York, I am well aware about coping with snowstorms. I remember a storm that in two days dumped over forty inches of snow on the area. Our plant was closed for two days, and dealing with the storm was a nice adventure and something my whole family will always remember. However years later in California, I encountered a storm that surpassed it in excitement and was even more unforgettable

That year we rented a house at the foot of a small ski area known as Tahoe Donner; our friends the Robbs came to spend the week skiing with us. One day as we left the North Star ski area, it started to snow. As we made our way up the hill to our house, the snow was coming down hard and the visibility was very poor; but we safely reached our house, which now resembled an igloo. The roof had several feet of snow on it, and the yard had drifts that left little room for light to pass through the windows. After dinner we played bridge and, through the narrowing gaps of visibility, watched the snow continue to fall. It felt so good to be embraced by the warmth and coziness of the house. We retired early because skiing does that to you.

When we awoke the next morning, the house seemed quite dark. The snow now engulfed the house, and each window appeared like the drapes were drawn over it. We turned on the radio and found over fifty inches had fallen and more was expected during the day. We were obviously not going anyplace. However, with a nice fire, a refrigerator full of food, a deck of cards, and good friends to share everything with, the day turned out to be quite pleasant.

Finally, late in the afternoon the snowstorm ended, and soon afterward a big Payloader appeared in our driveway; our rent included someone to plow. We went outside to observe the results of the storm. The house was no longer distinguishable. It now served as the base for a long sledding hill. As we noted our plowed driveway, down the street came a huge snowblower creating even higher banks to hide the houses. We found out later that over eighty inches had come down during the snowstorm. The powder-loving skiers would be in heaven while the rest of us hoped the groomers would pack down the slopes for us.

The next day we wanted to try and ski, but we wondered if the ski areas would be open. One of our friends suggested that the Sugar Bowl area was the place to go. It seemed rather odd since the place has the highest base lodge in north Tahoe, being located near the summit of the Route 80 pass. We first had to go down about 1500 feet from our house to reach the highway. Part of the road is quite steep, and with the hardpacked snow, a slow descent is necessary so as not to turn your car into a sled.

The area around Truckee is where a migrating wagon train known as the Donner party had so much trouble decades ago trying to survive a harsh and snowy winter. The most direct route to Sugar Bowl is to take the Donner Pass road, but this steep winding way was not a good choice after the storm. We were heading for the Route 80 summit, and then going to travel on old Highway 40. Traversing the summit is an impressive sight: you gaze upon huge rock formations and see many snow-covered peaks. However, when snow comes to the mountains, crossing the summit can be intimidating. State troopers stop you to make sure your vehicle can make it without being stranded. There was plenty of snow on the interstate, but it was plowed and we made good time. On this day, having a four-wheel-drive vehicle was considered adequate, but some days the troopers require you to also put chains on. Crossing the pass was easy compared to old Route 40. It had been plowed but was filled with deep ruts and mounds of snow, and my four-wheel-drive vehicle, with some difficulty, slowly made its way to the ski area.

When we were putting on our skis, we noticed people attaching long colorful cord between their boots and skis. Obviously this procedure was to aid you in locating your skis if they came off in the deep snow. We were planning to avoid ungroomed trails, so we didn't bother with this precaution. We headed for the Silver Belt chairlift, which took you to the 8400-foot Lincoln Peak. We assumed that the long intermediate trail back down the mountain would be groomed. The trip up was quite interesting; as we ascended we noticed the snow getting deeper because the chair came closer and closer to the snow. Near the peak, the snow rose above the cable supporting the chair. We then traveled through a half pipe that had been plowed out of the snow. When we got off the lift, we were happy to find the trail we planned to take down was packed. At the top we hesitated a moment to gaze on the blanket of snow that covered all the trees and rocks. It was a scene where everything was white. On the way down we noticed some people had tried unsuccessfully to negotiate the powder and were fishing their skis out of the snow. Others, who had no cords on their skis, had managed to secure metal detectors to search for their skis that had disappeared in the snow.

Near the bottom of the run, Doug Robb and I noticed a short stretch of untouched powder that looked inviting. We thought, why not give it a try? It was a mistake; with our standard skis and our lack of proper technique, we quickly sank up to our hips in snow. I stuck my pole in the snow to steady myself, but almost fell into the snow face-first because the pole never stopped sinking. I thought one could drown in this stuff. I quickly made a traverse across the hill to reach the packed trail, and Doug soon followed me. We had learned our lesson, and the rest of the day we confined ourselves to the groomed trails. The skiing was fantastic, plus you were in awe of the amount of snow surrounding you and gained such a respect for what Mother Nature is capable of.

After we safely returned home, I couldn't help thinking about and contrasting our day with the life-threatening experiences of the Donner party. We had encountered a storm of frightening intensity, but our circumstances allowed us to take advantage of what came down from the heavens for an unusual day of skiing.

In 1996, during the month of March, some good friends invited us to spend a week with them at Cancun. It was hard not to accept, so we compromised with ourselves by going to ski for a week with the Dohertys at Taos, New Mexico. The skiing was fine, but even better were the many nearby sightseeing opportunities, and we began to think maybe the lure of Lake Tahoe skiing was fading. We have not returned to ski there, but we have visited the area in the summer to celebrate Scott Bertz's wedding and for a family reunion. It will always be a special place for Yvonne and me.

After knowing the pleasures of skiing out west and not returning, our enthusiasm for the sport may have diminished slightly, but we did look forward each winter to hitting the slopes. We kept our membership at Labrador and confined our ski holidays to Vermont and western New York. Remembering Yvonne skiing down the Mardi Gras trail at the Holiday Valley resort singing an opera aria will always remind me of how much fun we have had with the sport. However, time and physical ailments started to take their toll. We each had a knee that gave us discomfort and obtained braces to help alleviate the problem. The situation became a little more complicated when Yvonne had her hip replaced in 1998 and I broke my leg in 2003 going to church during the winter. As a result, we each missed time skiing, but we always came back to try again. When Yvonne reached seventy, we switched to skiing at Toggenburg, where our age entitled us to ski free. Our braces didn't seem to help as much anymore, so we spent less time on the slopes and more time recuperating in the ski lodge. Finally, in 2005, I fell twice on one run trying to favor my knee: I normally wouldn't fall twice in two years. I decided it was time to put my skis away for good, and Yvonne felt the same way.

As you get older, it is always difficult to give up doing things that gave you so much enjoyment. But writing this piece reminded me of how much sharing skiing with our family and friends added to our happiness. Thriving on nice memories makes getter older so much easier.

A GRATIFYING CAREER ENDING

My professional experience prepared me for a challenging assignment at the end of my working career.

After receiving my master's degree in electrical engineering and teaching at the army's Air Defense Radar School and New York University, I went to work in 1956 for General Electric's heavy military electronics department in Syracuse, New York. I spent the next thirty-six years employed in a wide variety of engineering activities in their aerospace business, where large radar and sonar systems were the major product. While working at General Electric, I continued going to school, and in 1961 I received an MBA from Syracuse University. When I look back, I realize so many of my experiences were preparing me for my biggest professional challenge. It occurred just before my retirement when I was chosen for the position of technical director and the company's senior representative in a consortium called Euro-Art. Besides General Electric, it was comprised of Thorn EMI of England, Thomson CSF of France, and Siemens of Germany. The companies were embarking on the development of radar for locating mortar and artillery weapons; the project was being funded by the three European countries. My role in this program was a challenge that led to very satisfying results and a rewarding way to end my career.

As a young engineer I spent time designing electrical equipment and working in the lab, but I soon found it more interesting to develop designs and test them in the total radar system. During this period my most interesting and exciting assignment was as the system engineer on a very long-range tracking radar; its missions were to report on the position of objects circling the earth and to observe the flight of Russian test missiles. To complete my responsibilities, I had to work for seven months assisting in the installation and testing of the system in remote eastern Turkey. It was a thrill to see this radar with its eighty-four-foot-diameter antenna and high power transmitters performing its role of tracking space objects and gathering data following the launch of a Russian missile. For many years this system performed this important mission for the U.S. Air Force.

The work required me to be separated from my wife and three small children and labor long hours each day of the week. However, I was also able to become somewhat familiarized with the urban and isolated cultures of Turkey, while my family shared a unique bonding experience with their heritage by living in Italy. These pluses, along with a significantly higher salary, compensated somewhat for the long personal separation from my family. It was the start of my being introduced to cultures outside of the United States.

Upon my return, several assignments led to recognition of my engineering abilities and resulted in my appointment as a unit manager. This position is General Electric's lowest level of functional responsibility. You are assigned a group of technical personnel who you appoint to department projects, and then you help guide their activities. Periodically you evaluate their performance, which leads to determining their compensation. Your people are making a direct contribution to the particular project and will usually receive technical direction from a senior engineer or a program manager. Your position is mainly an advisory one.

I found at times I needed the satisfaction of a more direct involvement in department activities. So I made myself available to provide technical support to marketing personnel in their pursuit of new business. This often led to me having a key role in a proposal submission. A proposal is an intense activity that takes place over a short period of time and requires indentifying the many contributors and guiding their contributions. To help our department with this type of work, I was instrumental in hiring people with extensive experience in organizing and writing proposals. Their expertise taught me a lot about organizing large technical documents and getting engineers to make meaningful contributions. My newfound skill led to many requests for my participation in large study efforts, proposals, and technical reports.

Another somewhat different activity occurred when I was appointed to the department's International Technology Council; its charter was to investigate whether European and Japanese companies had technology that we could incorporate in our offerings to the U.S. military. I was asked to explore the Italian aerospace industries, and I made three trips to visit several leading companies. We flattered the companies with our interest, but we had little success in finding useful technologies. However, we did establish a presence in Europe, which made it easier to collaborate in future opportunities.

I spent several years juggling my functional responsibilities along with all the special assignments in which I was asked to participate. It was both flattering and exciting to contribute in so many different ways to the department's activities. I learned a great deal about motivating engineers, leading their contributions, and organizing their output. However, I felt somewhat overlooked for advancement opportunities and I wanted to seek a different challenge. I found it for a while working for a manager who was pursuing business opportunities in Europe.

At the time, NATO European countries were investigating their technology needs in defending themselves against their view of the Russian military threat. With my radar technical background, I was able to get myself included into several study efforts that were being undertaken. For almost a year I traveled to Europe about once a month to discuss requirements for their perceived needs and presented ideas for incorporating our department's technology. It was a stimulating undertaking since the Europeans' technical knowledge was impressive, but their marketing competiveness was somewhat lacking because each company often had government support for contracts within the country. Their approach to business was relaxed, and meals together were an important way of developing personal rapport.

During this time our department was developing a relationship with companies in England, France, and Germany who were interested in forming a consortium to pursue a development contract for an artillery-locating radar. At the time, Russia's vast arsenal of such weapons was considered a serious threat in European land warfare. The three European countries were pooling their monies to fund the effort. General Electric was invited to participate because we offered to provide some advanced solid-state technology for an antenna design that would provide the system with some very desirable features. I assisted in writing a proposal for the study phase of the program, and the governments awarded contracts to three different teams. Euro-Art assembled a study group in Munich, where they worked for eleven months and wrote a report and proposal that comprised over a thousand pages of information.

The international marketing manager to whom I was reporting had been working as the program manager for the study, and just a month prior to submitting the written material he asked me to go to Munich to write an executive summary for the report. It was the type of document common in the States, but the Europeans had no experience putting one together. I brought in a technical publications specialist from Thorn EMI in England and a conceptual artist from Thomson CSF in France. I formulated a number of topics in a storyboard format, listed what I knew about each one, and got the study team to comment and add things I overlooked. I then wrote text for storyboards and conceived artwork to accompany the material. The final document was twenty-eight pages long and covered all aspects of the study, but in a very concise way with bulleted statements and impressive visuals to aid in making a point. Euro-Art was selected to start negotiating the development contract, and we were told that the executive summary was the thing that tipped the award in our favor. It was an intense, demanding effort over a three-week period, but it gave me a great sense of satisfaction and I was proud of what I had accomplished.

Throughout the study and through the evaluation period, the companies were deciding and negotiating how they would work together. One of the things they specified was to form a program office to interface with the customer. It would be staffed with a managing director to be provided by Thomson; and reporting to him would be a commercial director who would be a Thorn man, a program manager who would come from Siemens, and a technical director from General Electric. The French and German customers were each supplying 40 percent of the funding, and since the program office was to be in Munich, Thomson was assigned the higher-ranking position to offset the location advantage.

I immediately thought the technical director's position was an ideal opportunity for me. I was fifty-eight years old at the time, and the job would be a great and meaningful way to end my career with General Electric. I wrote a short resume that showed how much pertinent experience I had for the position, and I received the approval from the companies' management representatives.

The first part of the program consisted of writing and negotiating three documents that were normally issued with the request for proposals, namely: the contract definition requirements, the statement of work, and the technical specifications. Every time we complained that a requirement was not included in our quote, they hinted that they would have to consider talking to another team. A government group that once was considered somewhat naive and inexperienced was turning out to be quite shrewd.

After signing a contract we were able to bring aboard supporting personnel to help perform our primary program functions of being the sole interface with the customer and making sure all consortium members were aware of what each one was doing. All design activities were performed by the companies; but since we reviewed each document that went to the customer, we were able to suggest changes if we anticipated any problems. Since most interfaces with the customer were technical in nature, I received approval for six engineering people to help me.

The system engineering effort to which all companies had to assign people was being done in Paris under Thomson's direction, and either I or a member of my staff would attend meetings there to keep up-to-date and offer suggestions where appropriate. There were also quarterly meetings to brief the company's senior management members of the program's progress. Then every time we submitted something to the customer, there were questions to be answered either in writing or by making trips to his offices in Koblenz.

However, the thing that kept me most busy was guiding and leading the companies through a series of milestone reviews at which the customer would evaluate your progress, ask questions, and possibly suggest changes to your work. These are common customer activities in the United States; but the Europeans added the stipulation that if the review was not satisfactory, no progress payments were to be made. This placed added emphasis and stress on each review. These types of exchanges were new activities for both the customer and the European companies, and there was a learning process for them in conducting them. In the beginning of the contract, the milestones required the participation of all consortium companies since they involved continual scrutiny of all aspects of the design in finer and finer detail. These reviews occurred every three or four months and occupied three or four days of in-depth technical discussions. The meetings were attended by a large group of technical experts from the three nations and many of the engineering staff of Euro-Art. The review was followed by time to discuss if we had met the criteria for approval, and it was always necessary to answer in writing the many questions that were raised at the meeting. You can see why I spent so much of my time preparing for and responding to these reviews.

We were on time for every scheduled review and never missed getting our contract payment approved. Preparing and attending these meetings was a benefit not only for the customer, but also for Euro-Art because the companies kept abreast of what progress was being made on the program and they were able to appreciate the contribution of the program office.

My role in conducting these reviews allowed me to become involved with most members of the consortium. Working with the engineers on my staff or the ones working at company locations never presented any difficulties. Their first priority was to the program and satisfying its technical requirements.

Achieving a solution to a difficult situation and having to cope with the differences in cultural backgrounds made the problem-solving process somewhat interesting. A lot of time was spent talking about languages and how difficult it was for the French and German associates to be properly understood. In fact, at times this difficulty even extended to American and English exchanges. You did not fully appreciate this problem until you had spent several months in a multicultural environment.

The fact that the official language of the consortium was British English instead of American English was usually not a problem, but sometimes confusion was created. A prime example at an early meeting was the use of the expression "to table an issue." To an American, it means to remove an item from further discussion; while for the British, it means just the opposite, to bring an item to the table. It was quite amusing discovering and straightening out the misunderstanding. The differences between these two languages are many, and you need to be able to recognize them and adapt yourself. When a person translates from his first language to another one, the differences can become even greater. The German director was always using the word "aggressive" to describe people. I pointed out that saying a person is aggressive is usually a negative way to describe someone. He gave a surprised look and said, "In German, it can mean one who is dynamic and very confident."

Even the styles of speaking and writing in the same language varied between cultures. A French customer complained once that American writing was very direct and to the point, while English explanations were considered too long. What he was looking for was a more expressive, flowery, and polite form that is typical of Italian and French writing.

When engineers from different cultures were brought together to jointly solve problems, they essentially functioned as part of a single company. Still, there were differences in how each culture operated. The Americans and English are a bit more imaginative, the French a bit harder working, and the Germans definitely more thorough. The program managers of each company had to deal with many nontechnical and commitment issues as well as making technical progress, so cooperation between them was often more difficult to achieve. The focus of their efforts was to protect their companies. The management group was better able to place program priorities above company interests. In fact, that was their job, but they often received criticism from their companies when they became too objective.

Within the program office I developed good rapport with the managing director, Michel, and a lot of it was due to our wives getting along so well. The women had a unique way of communicating; since they both spoke each other's language, it was easier for them to speak in their native tongue and listen in the other. Michel knew English well, but when we were all together, which was quite often, it made him more comfortable to occasionally lapse into French. He valued my technical knowledge and leadership contributions to the program, and I gained an appreciation for his tactfulness in handling the companies and the customer. Our relationship grew into one of respect and fondness for one another. I also enjoyed working with Dennis, the commercial director, although our paths didn't often cross at work. His sense of humor often led to relieving the tension in a meeting, and our wives became good friends. My wife Yvonne's upbringing, her language skills, and earlier trips to Europe made her comfortable dealing with Europeans. In addition, she felt that she was representing the United States, and this made her extra sensitive when interacting with people.

I managed to develop a good personal relationship with all members of our program staff because I made them partners in addressing a problem. In Europe and England—as I saw on my earlier visits to NATO countries—there is a tendency for the boss to maintain a detachment. Of course, playing tennis with some of them also helped in developing empathy. I remember a young Frenchman, who worked for the program director, called me at home. He said he had left the keys to his apartment at his parents' home when he visited them in Paris and he was locked out. He wanted me to help him somehow break into his apartment. I didn't think that was a good idea, and I suggested he stay at my place while he waited for his parents to mail him the keys. I think he was surprised by the offer, but he accepted it and we all spent a very pleasant time together. He later sent my wife a beautiful bouquet of flowers.

The only association problem we all had was with the German program director, Manfred. He was a bachelor, much younger than the other directors, and a good-looking fellow who was fun to socialize with. Yvonne and I enjoyed his company, and for most of the time we were good friends. However, as we progressed in our work, his professional ego, which was not supported by significant job contributions, began to affect our relationship and we drifted apart. There was also a conflict between his role and that of the managing director, and I believe he thought he could usurp the director's position, but it never happened. At times his negative attitude and his tendency to favor our customer's position on issues disrupted meetings. I know when I was there, the managing director unsuccessfully tried to get him replaced. I understand that soon after I left, my successor and Manfred stopped speaking to each other. However, during my time on the program, Manfred's performance was a minor issue and Euro-Art's board of senior managers was pleased with the program's progress.

I left the program when we received final approval for all our specifications and overall drawings; this was referred to as the critical design review. At this time detailed agreement had been achieved on what would be built and tested. Yvonne and I had been away from family and friends for four years, and we felt it was time to return home. However, it was really dull going to work in Syracuse after spending four years addressing the challenges at Euro-Art; so five months after I returned, I retired from GE.

Shortly afterward, I received a call from Euro-Art's marketing people, who asked me if I would write a technical brochure for them. It sounded like an interesting opportunity and a good way to make a transition into retirement. I enlisted the support of a creative publications specialist; and I made one trip to Munich to collect information, and a second visit to obtain final approval for the document. The thirty-page brochure described the challenges of solving the weapon location problem and the uniqueness of Euro-Art's approach. Everyone was pleased with the document.

Through occasional phone conversations and a personal trip to Europe, I was able to keep in touch with the consortium's progress. The technical achievements were very noteworthy. Advanced sophisticated radar was delivered to the English, French, and German governments as scheduled, and it met very stringent performance requirements. After many years of study and negotiation, the companies and the countries arrived at an agreement to enter into a multimillion-dollar contract for producing twenty-five systems.

Company rivalries and cultural differences usually make it difficult for international cooperative ventures to be successful. Euro-Art participants had their share of bickering, frustrations, and mistakes, but somehow well-defined commitments and mutual interest kept progress on track. Diversity of opinions and attitudes can often be a detriment to achievement; but if they are properly harnessed and focused, they can help a project succeed. Having played an important role in the program's accomplishments continues to give me a fond recollection of my most demanding professional undertaking.

LIVING IN MUNICH

Life in Munich was a time that we always recall with much fondness.

As I reviewed events in my life, I found there was no time that offered more challenges and rewards than the period that Yvonne and I spent living in Munich. Encountering another culture as a tourist is quite different from the experience of trying to become a resident in a foreign environment. I have written a great deal about these years in an earlier book, but I felt my current recollections would not be complete without some reflection on this very exciting period.

Previous to settling in Munich, I had traveled for several years in Europe on different assignments for General Electric, so I was aware of some of the diversity in living that can exist in a foreign country. Yvonne had even more exposure to life abroad with her teenage visits to Italy with her parents, studying at an Italian university, and living with our three small children in Ivrea. In addition, I also managed at times to take her with me when I traveled overseas. An advantage Yvonne had in adapting to the European environment was her ability to speak both Italian and French. Also, prior to settling in Munich, I had learned some things about the city. I had spent three weeks in the city on a special assignment and had brought Yvonne with me on a couple of other occasions.

All of this exposure to foreign travel made both of us knowledgeable about some of the dissimilarities in lifestyle we might encounter in living overseas. However, trying to make a home in Europe presents problems and challenges that a visitor does not usually come across.

The company did try to help in making the transition by sending us to a three-day course introducing us to German culture. They also hired an agent to assist in getting through the formal processing in establishing our residency and to aid in finding an apartment. Although this assistance gave us some comfort, we really felt we were on our own in trying to adapt.

General Electric was reasonably generous in providing financial support. They winterized our home in Syracuse, installed a security system, and allowed us to hire someone to occasionally start our automobiles. When I went to Germany, they raised my salary by 20 percent, leased a car for me, paid for the rent and the furnishing of an apartment, and gave me a per diem for incidental expenses. I was satisfied with the financial package, but noticed that the directors sent to Germany from other companies received even more generous compensation.

The first chore in living in another country is finding a place to live. It is a time-consuming activity, and we avoided residing in a hotel while looking by staying in a nice resident hotel called the Stollberg Plaza. It had a bedroom, a living room, a small kitchen, and underground parking. Each day they brought a substantial breakfast to our room, and later in the day someone came in to clean the apartment. We were in the center of the city and close to many stores and restaurants, so it was a convenient and interesting location to begin becoming familiar with Munich.

There are few furnished apartments in Munich, so we decided to try and rent an unfurnished residence. Except for the bathroom, these dwellings contained only the four walls and no closets. I will never forget when I asked an agent showing me an apartment where the kitchen was. He took me into a room with two pipes coming out of the wall.

There are many nice areas to live in Munich, and we decided we wanted to combine urban and suburban living by looking for a place located near the English Gardens. The site is a magnificent large park that extends from downtown to the city limits in the north. It contains paved tree-lined paths for walking and bike riding that take you past large grassy lawns and alongside the gentle flowing Isar River, which runs through the park. When you feel the need for refreshments, there are three beer gardens to take care of your wants. One beer garden sits beside a large lake that adds to the ambiance.

After several disappointing searches, we found through our own initiative just what we were looking for. The apartment was on the first floor and had a large foyer leading to a living room with an eating area, a kitchen, a small bedroom, and a hall that led to two more bedrooms and two bathrooms. A door in the living room opened up onto a small patio that led to a path into the English Gardens. Finding the apartment presented us some difficulties, but now we had the bigger challenge of filling it with furniture. Fortunately, the previous tenant was willing to sell us the kitchen in the apartment, so our task was made a little simpler.

Shopping in Munich was not too convenient since the only time I could go with Yvonne when the stores were open was after work on Thursday and Saturday morning. However, there were a couple of stores open on Sundays for browsing, so we would wander around them trying to figure what was being offered and how much it would cost. After a lot of hard work over a couple of weekends, we had a list of what we might buy. Then I took one day off from work, and Yvonne and I and my German-speaking secretary went out to make our purchases. Besides cost, timely delivery was an important criterion; and after a number of considered decisions, we spent quite a bit of money and bought enough furnishings to make the apartment livable. That day was a rather unusual one for Yvonne and me; we walked into the store owning nothing and walked out with a houseful of essential furnishings. Over the next several months we continued shopping, and we added several more items to make the apartment even more habitable. We were proud of the comfortable home that we eventually created.

The next task in adapting to living in a foreign country is making friends and developing a social life. When we arrived in Munich, I knew only two other directors who were working out of our office at a Siemens plant; Yvonne knew no one. In the beginning I was spending a lot of time working in Koblenz, so Yvonne was left alone, which made her exceedingly unhappy. On several occasions I took her to Koblenz, where she could spend time with Ella, the English director's wife, and Jane, a General Electric contract administrator's spouse. It was a real treat for Yvonne to interact with these women.

Before Yvonne came to Munich, I overheard in a restaurant a couple speaking perfect German to a waitress and English to each other. I was curious and went over and introduced myself. Soon I discovered that Hans worked for General Dynamics, and for years Marianna had been a teacher in California. They were a part of a small team of Americans working with the Germans on a joint venture project, and they offered to give me the names of some people to contact when I settled in Munich. Soon after moving in, I discovered that two couples on the team (the Bartons and the Comings) lived in our apartment complex; we now had neighbors we knew. One day on the bus Yvonne met Patty Ryan and discovered she was also a neighbor. Our social circle was beginning to expand, and each one of these couples became good friends.

When I started to work in Munich, a member of our skeleton staff was the managing director, Michel Fermi. He was French and married with three children. I almost immediately began to develop a relationship that eventually became very close. Yvonne's command of French helped greatly in the development of a bond. I was fascinated by the relationship between Michel's wife, Arlette, and Yvonne. When they were together, Arlette would speak to Yvonne in French and Yvonne would respond in English. It made conversation for each of them much less stressful.

We went together on volksmarches, played bridge, went out to dinner, cross-country skied, and entertained each other in our homes. Their enthusiasm for all things French enhanced our appreciation for the culture, especially their wines and cheeses. The friendship continued by visiting one another even after we returned home. Michel, a modest and reserved person, paid us what I am sure for a French person is a rare compliment when he told us that they considered us like family. When Arlette's untimely death occurred a few years ago, we felt a great loss, and we tried to ease Michel's sorrow through correspondence with him.

When a contract was finally negotiated, our staff significantly increased, and there were many more people for me to interact with each day. One in particular was Dennis Bailey, the commercial director who, with his wife Ella, moved into our apartment complex. Dennis and I would at times share rides into work, and Yvonne had another woman to share her day with. Their good humor and graciousness seemed typical of English behavior and made spending time with them very pleasant. We became good friends, and even after leaving the project would visit each other. Seeing one another in our home settings made our friendship grow into something special. Even after Dennis passed away, Ella kept in touch and visited with us on a couple of occasions.

The relationships with the Fermis and the Baileys started as business associations and grew with time into friendships that allowed each of us to gain insights into each other's cultures. These insights created memories that erased the sorrow caused by the deaths of the spouses.

Once the contract officially started, my responsibilities increased considerably, but interaction with the staff made life professionally and socially fulfilling. There were important meetings and milestones successfully completed, friendly lunches eaten in Siemens's excellent cafeteria, tennis matches played on Munich's wonderful clay courts, and office parties to celebrate each other's birthdays. One disappointment was my inability to understand the game of cricket; I had watched an associate play the game and his wife tried, without success, to explain it to me.

When we traveled through the English Gardens, we often met people we knew, and it made us feel at home. The occasion that made me feel even more pleased occurred when Yvonne organized a surprise party for my sixtieth birthday. I entered our apartment and was greeted by a large crowd, all drinking champagne and toasting my becoming a senior citizen. I truly realized that Munich had become a new home for me.

Adding to our feeling of well-being was an English-speaking German doctor whose treatment of us could be a model of behavior for our American doctors. He gave a full half-hour of his time by first examining you and then discussing his diagnosis in his office. When you left he saw you to his door, bid you good-bye, and helped put on your coat. Yvonne still follows the hypertension regime he developed for her.

An activity we found to be quite varied and enjoyable was going to church on Sunday. There was the German mass in a church with a sanctified ambiance and an inspiring choir, but no homily message we understood. It was a short walk from our house, and we did become friendly with a couple who lived in the States and was retiring in Germany. Then there was the mass conducted by Irish priests studying at a German seminary. The services were quite informal, the sermons were excellent, and the coffee and doughnuts afterward made for a very friendly start to the day. When we had reason to go to the army base in Munich, we enjoyed the American-like mass at the chapel.

Little things can make a big difference in your life—such as discovering we could have the *Stars and Stripes* newspaper delivered to our door each day. This meant we could read the paper in the morning while we sipped our coffee, and on Sunday we could read it in bed. It was a habit we had grown accustomed to at home. Another added benefit was that the army paper was truly like an American newspaper, unlike all English-language newspapers in Europe that focused on continental news.

Munich is an interesting and exciting place to live. It has world-class museums and opera, fine restaurants, spectacular shopping, beautiful parks, and an extensive transportation system to make it easy to get around. Our only criticism is that the weather can be damp and rainy at times and a bit cold in the winter. However, if the sun comes out in the winter, the beer gardens in the English Gardens are always ready to open up. I remember drinking beer sitting at a table resting on the ice in the lake, and nearby were people playing the game of curling.

We had a TV set to watch when we needed to stay indoors, but except for an English channel with awful old movies and exciting snooker matches and a German channel broadcasting the *Golden Girls* in English, there wasn't much to watch. However, there was a store that rented English movie videos, and when people went home they often returned with videos they would exchange, so TV watching was an entertainment option. In addition, there was also the alternative of going to one of the three theaters that showed English-language movies.

Besides Munich being a great place to live in, it was conveniently located close to many nearby attractions. Soon after we came to the city, we bought a book, *50 Day Trips in Germany*, and many places were an easy drive from Munich. Before we left the country, we had taken thirty-seven of the trips suggested, and in our travels discovered other places we frequently visited. It was also a short drive to the Austrian mountains, where there were numerous skiing opportunities, and the nearby interesting city of Salzburg. We never lacked for someplace to go on the weekends.

During the time we were in Munich, many people visited us and we enjoyed showing them how much the area had to offer. We had our family pass through going and coming from Larry's wedding, friends from Italy, and numerous visitors from the States. Since I was working, it was sometimes difficult to entertain them, but we always managed to show them a good time. Yvonne loved giving everyone a tour of Munich, and we would borrow bikes to give them the full pleasure of properly seeing the English Gardens. There were day tours to nearby cities, and sometimes we made extended stays into Italy with our guests. However, other times we put them on a train and sent them to Paris or Vienna. After all, fending for oneself is part of the experience of seeing Europe.

One visit from our Italian friends presented us with a special problem. The Cesare family consisted of four children, a brother-in-law and his wife, and a grandmother. We had shared several meals with the whole family and invited them to come see us, not expecting they might all arrive at once. One week they called us, saying they wanted to come up for Oktoberfest and they would bring Yvonne's mother with them. We did not want to discourage them and set about trying to make accommodations for them. We had room for the married couples in our apartment, and the Bartons offered to house the two grandmothers. Fortunately, Paul Comings was going to be away for the weekend, and he offered his place for the four children. They told us later they expected to have several people sleep on the floor. Cesare and his family, at the time, lived in a small three-bedroom apartment, so crowded conditions were something they were accustomed to. We were so glad we could make them comfortable, and they were very pleasantly surprised by our arrangements when they arrived.

They came in two cars on Friday and were planning to leave on Sunday. That night, though it was chilly, we took them to eat by the water of the Kleinhesselohen beer garden. Yvonne made a rolled turkey breast dish, and we complemented it with typical beer-garden fare: German potato salad, and lots of soft pretzels called bretzen, beer, and wine. It wasn't a standard Italian fare, but everyone seemed satisfied.

The next day after breakfast we headed for the Oktoberfest, and it was a day I won't easily forget. Besides beer, the other thing they have plenty of at this carnival is people. The beer tents and streets connecting them are jammed with hordes of mankind, all looking to have a good time. I felt like the pied piper leading our troop around and trying not to lose anyone, and my neck got sore keeping track of everyone.

By late afternoon we all were tired and we returned to our apartment, which gave us time to prepare the evening dinner. We managed to bring together all the tables and chairs we owned and our largest tablecloth in order to set up a banquet table with a place for everyone. We had prepared for a typical Italian feast with plenty of wine. At times we felt like hotel managers and tour guides, but we could tell that the whole family enjoyed themselves. There was never a dull moment, and it was very rewarding and an unforgettable weekend.

Yvonne had many English-speaking friends in her social circle, but there was a group of German and French women she associated with that really gave her a wonderful feeling of fulfillment. These women got together once a month to socialize and speak to each other in Italian. Yvonne's knowledge of Italian and French allowed her to readily participate in their conversations; she always returned from these meetings excited and stimulated. They talked about families, their lifestyles, world politics, and their personal philosophies; Yvonne said they were well-read and interesting women. She was the only American in the group and worked hard at projecting a good image for our country. Providing coffee and sweets for the ladies was a challenge because three luscious homemade desserts were necessary to show your guests a proper offering. When Yvonne was hostess she prepared three typical American desserts—apple pie, frosted brownies, and chocolate chip cookies. They were not the usual lavish desserts, but everyone loved them and eagerly asked for the recipes. Yvonne developed a special relationship with one of the women and has maintained the friendship through letter and card writing and recently by e-mail. Yvonne's background made it easy for her to fit in with these European women, and she was proud of the ready acceptance they gave her.

There were so many things that left lasting impressions on us while we lived in Munich. For years after we returned, we would reminisce about events that occurred; and though some memories have faded, reading my earlier book brings them to life again. I returned twice after I left, and once Yvonne came with me. She often said she wished we had a timeshare in Munich where each year we could renew our association with the city. However, since all our friends have left, I am sure things would be quite different.

It is probably best to remember it as a time in our life when we were ready and able to accept and deal with the myriad of events we encountered and enjoy the outcomes they produced.

Sustaining Family Connections

Throughout my life special efforts were made to maintain family ties.

The family is sometimes referred to as an institution, because it is an entity with a social and educational purpose. Carrying out this function depends on the connections that are established within the family. Over time these connections may be harder to maintain because distance and mobility can reduce contact and affect the bonding process. Early in my life, I probably took my family for granted and went my own way. After getting married, my attitude began to change, and I realized that the family can be a lasting association if you make the effort to sustain the link.

In growing up with my siblings, my relationship with them was not personally close. My sister was eighteen months younger than I, but somehow being a girl seemed to limit our hanging out together. My brother was five years younger, and that made our early years of socializing difficult. However, our parents always made us feel like a close family because we ate most meals together and we all celebrated holidays with our relatives. We attended the same grammar school, but we started to become separated when it came time to enter high school. I applied and was accepted at Brooklyn Technical High School, which offered several courses not given at other city schools. It meant I had to travel by subway for an hour each day to attend classes. My brother and sister attended Bryant High School, a short bus ride from home.

I am not sure what type of interaction represents typical sibling behavior, but my conduct probably wouldn't win me any prizes for being a model big brother. I associated with friends from school or the boys at the nearby park, while my brother and sister went their own ways. My wife, Yvonne, who was an only child and longed for a brother or sister, could not understand my lack of attachment. Maybe sleeping in the same room or in the same bed with my brother fostered a need for other relationships.

I went on to college and saw my teenage friends less as I spent most times with my school associates. My sister went to work after high school, and my brother began to distinguish himself as a high school athlete. He was good enough to be awarded a scholarship to St. John's University. During this time we lived in a three-bedroom apartment that was a remodeled funeral parlor. It was a lot roomier than our past living quarters, but with only one small bathroom, mornings became quite hectic. Living together was quite harmonious, but my brother and sister and I still did very little socializing with each other. After college I was drafted into the army and sent to El Paso, Texas, and my sister married, so my brother was the only one left at home. When he finished college, he was drafted and shipped to Japan for his tour of duty.

Over the years I began to realize that friends came into your life and were quite important to you, but these relationships were soon broken up by moving or different career paths, and soon your only connection was a yearly Christmas card. However, my family was always there to lend support or celebrate an event, and though meetings may have been infrequent, I felt each occasion showed that family was a special kind of bond.

Each of us made our contribution to an expanding society. I had three children, my sister four, and my brother three, but living far apart from one another made getting together a little difficult. One year my brother suggested we try to spend a week vacationing with all the cousins. He knew where my sister and I could rent a large house on a lake near his home in Sturbridge, Massachusetts. My wife, I, and our three children joined my sister and her four children and my father for a week. The house had a lot of rooms, but it was a bit rustic and had only one bathroom. After it rained for four days, we ran out of parlor games and discovered that the roof leaked. When the sun finally came out, my father got nervous watching the children play in the lake; seven kids can do that to you. The somewhat rundown conditions made the week somewhat of a disappointment for the grown-ups, but the cousins enjoyed playing with each other. However, many years passed before we all got together again. During that time we made occasional visits to each other's homes, but each of us mainly focused on our own families.

The year my son Larry entered Bucknell University, we discovered that the school had student apartments for rent during the summer for very reasonable rates. So we planned many family reunions. The units had two bedrooms, with a space between them large enough for a bathroom, a lounging area, a dining table, and a small kitchen. The adults had a room for themselves and enough space to accommodate other family members. At that time, my children and my sister's children were old enough to have summer jobs and be left at home, so they came down when they could get away, usually on the weekend. My brother's three children were in high school, so they all came along. During the day we had access to campus tennis courts and a swimming pool. In the evening we had long cocktail hours while preparing a simple dinner for everyone. At night, games of charades and Trivial Pursuit gave us all a chance to find expression for our competitive spirits. We met like that for five years, and all the cousins got a chance to see each other. Later, we found accommodations on the New Jersey shore to house us, and for three more years we were able to get many of us together. However, the cousins started to get married, and reunions were limited to wedding celebrations.

There was a period in my life just before I retired when maintaining connections with my own family became somewhat difficult because I accepted an assignment working in Munich, Germany. Over the four years I was there, Yvonne and I managed through weekly phone calls and occasional visits home to not lose touch with our children. Each week we spent a long time talking with one of them on the phone; and they would, in turn, fill in the others. We would return home each Christmas and spend part of the holidays together.

Larry's wedding in Italy was a very special occasion for a wonderful family celebration. Our son Ray and daughter Susan, along with her husband Rose and their three children, Teddy, Mandy, and Alex came; all spent time with us and did sightseeing in Italy and Germany. At one point we returned to Munich with the three little ones and had a few days to spoil them. It was a wonderful opportunity for developing family attachments.

In my last year of being in Munich, I had several thousand frequent flyer miles with Pan Am that I would have had difficulty using. I thought my sister, who had never been out of the States, would welcome the opportunity to see Europe for the first time. I managed to get my points transferred so that she and her very good friend, Maryanne, could travel to Munich. Maryanne was the ideal traveling companion because she had family in Germany that they could visit and she could speak German. We spent almost a week showing them the sights of Munich before we headed south to Italy.

At our first stop in Mantua, we visited several tourist attractions, but what really impressed my sister was how the whole town seemed to turn out on a

Sunday evening to just walk around or sip some coffee and chat. She felt she was part of a celebration. Our next stop, at a lovely small inn just outside of Florence, allowed us to explore many of the appealing places in the region. Two days marveling at the art in Florence, a day experiencing the charm of Siena and San Gimignano, and another time holding up the leaning tower of Pisa for pictures were experiences that gave my sister a sample of Italian appeal. However, the most enjoyable visit appeared to be the day we discovered the unique area known as the Cinque Terre. It has steep slopes filled with grape arbors, cliffside villages overlooking the Mediterranean, and sandy beaches allowing us to bask in the sun; it all left a lasting impression. I enjoyed the wonder and pleasure I saw on my sister's face, which at times turned to tears when she realized the experiences she was deriving from her trip.

Several years later I took my brother and his wife, Rita, on a grand tour of many well-known tourist attractions in Italy. Yvonne and I had been in Italy for a while and picked them up at the Milan Airport. To ease their transition into the country, we spent a couple days relaxing in the beauty and tranquility of Lago di Garda. The visit might have been the highlight of the tour; of course, the wines we bought in Bardolino and drank each evening may have contributed to our favorable impression. Then it was on to the narrow crowded streets of Venice and its distinctive lifestyle. Our journey continued with stops at the Uffizi Museum in Florence and the Basilica of St. Francis in Assisi, and Rita's desire to see Italian art was more than fulfilled. Lunch at the famed Il Campo in Siena, which is surrounded by several palaces and is considered the greatest square in Italy, enhanced our appetite and appreciation for Italian history. On the way to Rome we drove up the steep winding road to Orvieto, and after finding a place to park the car, we walked about its narrow streets exploring the town. After lunch, we had difficulty finding our automobile.

I selected a small inn in the Rome suburbs for our stay in the city because it made housing our car easier. Besides, riding public transportation gave us a different view of the city. The contrast between the ruins and decay of the Colosseum and the opulence of St. Peter's Cathedral demonstrated for everyone Rome's impact on western civilization. The day before putting Marty and Rita on the plane for home, we visited the site of the allied landing at Anzio and treated ourselves to a wonderful Italian Sunday dinner. The appetite we observed of two nearby diners encouraged my brother and sister-in-law to make a feast of their last Italian meal in Italy.

Yvonne and I at one time thought about taking people on tours of Italy, but we found that the responsibility of carrying out plans and accommodating the wishes of people can often be taxing, so we gave up on the idea.

When my brother retired at the early age of fifty-five, he moved to Melbourne, Florida, and for a while he owned both a townhouse and a ranch house with a swimming pool. It was an opportunity for my sister and me to spend some time in the area. Yvonne and I made short visits, either staying in the townhouse or renting a condo on the ocean. One year we rented two condo units for our family, and everyone came down to spend Christmas together. It was the first time we had all seen Christmas lights on palm trees. My sister would stay most of the winters there; and after getting married again, she found a house she liked and moved her residence from Long Island to Melbourne. The place now became a family gathering locale. Since Yvonne and I were still skiing, we paid a visit for only a few weeks in March. However, it was always a great time for family ties to be renewed.

In 2003, the clan started by my parents spanned three generations and included forty-three parents and cousins. Some of us talked about having a reunion; and through the efforts of my son Larry and his wife, Blair, we assembled in Westfield, New Jersey, for a weekend of eating, drinking, playing, and reminiscing. The only ones missing were my brother's son, Robert, and his family. His work took him to Iraq, but he called and talked to most everyone present.

On Friday evening we all had dinner at a local restaurant, and on Saturday it was hero sandwiches at a nearby park followed by a softball game. (Some of us showed our age by having a person run for us after being fortunate enough to hit the ball!) That evening, a catered barbecue at Larry's house allowed cousins and parents to connect. The next day we returned to Larry and Blair's house to enjoy bagels and coffee. It was obvious everyone had a good time, and we talked about all of us soon getting together again, but it was years before it would happen. However, we each left with a memento of our time together: a T-shirt with each person's name listed on a family tree.

The following year my wife and I decided that we would get our own family together. At the time we were a coast-to-coast group. Susan lived in San Jose, California, Ray in Kansas City, and Larry in New Jersey. We decided that meeting at Lake Tahoe, California, would be a convenient vacation spot. Yvonne and I had spent part of three winters there, and my daughter could drive to the location. We flew Larry and Ray's family to Reno and rented a couple of cars to drive up the mountain to Truckee.

The house we rented was very comfortable and could sleep all sixteen. It turned out to be an idyllic week. The sun each day raised the afternoon temperature to the eighties, and nights cooled to a comfortable sixty degrees.

Ray had two young boys, so he had to break away from us at times; but we all had breakfast together, and at night each family took turns preparing dinner, which we ate around a huge dining table. A couple of nights, Yvonne and I felt it would be easier for us to take everyone to eat at a local restaurant. One day most of us went rafting down a rather gentle stretch of rapids in the Truckee River, and on another day some of us went hiking partway up the mountain at Squaw Valley. Larry and Rose, Susan's husband, showed off their youthful vigor by biking up and down the Donner Pass, a rather formidable undertaking. Larry also kept in shape by running in the woods, but curtailed this activity when he ran across a bear. Four of us spent a day playing on a plush golf course whose lush fairways were surrounded by dense woods, but fortunately we encountered no bears. Picnicking on the shores of Lake Tahoe was a perfect spot for everyone to enjoy the sun, water, and food. Every day seemed to offer some activity for us to take advantage of the pleasant weather and being with each other.

For several years we tried to think of other ways to get together again with our children. Since one family had college-age children and another had three girls approaching their teens, and my youngest son had his three boys beginning school, the task was not easy. Finally, we thought an ideal getaway that promised fun for such a diverse family was a Disney cruise. We flew all seventeen of us—Ray had added another boy to his tribe—into Orlando, the tour bus took us to the embarkation port at Cape Canaveral, and we set forth for four days in the capable hands of the Disney staff. We spent two days on Disney's private island enjoying the sun, sand, and water and one morning exploring the town of Nassau, but mostly we enjoyed being pampered by the abundance and variety of the ship's food, the first class entertainment, and other myriad activities. Everyone could seek his own pleasures, but we were often together to share in what was being offered. One evening was especially memorable when all the adults gathered for an exceptional dinner, while all the cousins roamed the ship together. Times had changed because, instead of buying Susan's children ice cream, I was now treating them to drinks. The young ones questioning when we were going to go on a cruise again and the happy smiles on everyone's faces gave Yvonne and me the greatest satisfaction.

The bonding wasn't over because plans had been made for some from my brother's and sister's families to be in Melbourne on the weekend after we returned from our cruise. Many of us stayed at the same hotel, where we had cocktails, dined, and afterward played charades in the lobby. On a second day, we had a swim party and casual catered dinner at my sister's community pool.

A baseball cap with a large D and palm tree embroidered on it gave everyone a keepsake for our time with each other. We hoped that times like this gave all participants memories that they will reflect on in the future.

Since Yvonne and I gave up skiing, Melbourne has become a place where we go for three months during the winter. Each of us siblings has our own social activities, but there are frequent opportunities to get together. What is especially nice is when our children visit and they get to meet their aunts and uncles and, on occasion, even their cousins. We love Syracuse, but escaping it in the winter to enjoy Florida's weather, and being able at the same time to have the additional benefit of family activities, makes the winter even more pleasurable.

As you can see, my wife and I have made an effort to maintain family ties in spite of the distances that separate us from our kin. We often envy our friends who have their family in the area and can share so many more of the events and moments in their lives. However, maybe separation reduces the chances of problems and minor irritations and makes each meeting something to remember and cherish. We accept our situation and are grateful for the moments when we can make connections.

OUR CHILDREN'S WEDDINGS

*Each of our three children had such interesting stories associated
with their weddings that I felt compelled to write about the events.*

The weddings of your children are events every parent can never forget. We
are the proud parents of three children whose weddings we remember with
great fondness, especially since each of them made the occasion a completely
different type of experience for us. Our involvement with them prior to the
event helped in establishing a family bond and made the ceremonies unusually
poignant.

Susan

My daughter was a recent graduate from Clarkson College and working
in the Washington DC. area for GE as an engineer in a large information
technology storage facility. She met and started dating Roosevelt Bynum,
who had attended Annapolis and the University of Maryland and worked
as a programmer for the company. We had been with them when they were
together, and it was obvious that the relationship was becoming a serious
one. Although Rose was a fine young man, Yvonne and I had a grave concern
about the association since he was black. Neither of us really knew well
any black people, but we felt that we were not prejudiced toward them. We
are both from New York City and had associated with and accepted many
different ethnic cultures, but they were all Caucasian. All we knew about
Afro-Americans we learned from the media, which is not a good source for
understanding them. Our attitude toward them was passive and neutral, but
we knew that many others didn't share our way of thinking. Our concern
for our daughter and her future happiness made us seek the outlook of other
people. We felt a marriage could be difficult enough without introducing a
racial issue to complicate it.

We expressed our strong reservations to Susan about her plans, but we soon realized that it was her life and we could help her confront any additional burdens she would be taking on by being completely supportive of what she wanted to do. We felt that our daughter understood our initial concern and embraced our new attitude. We then started preparing and looking forward to a formal church wedding and reception several months in the future.

Waiting out this period and sharing apartments with associates was unappealing to Susan and Rose, and the desire to have a place of their own to begin their marriage started them looking for a house. They found a place that suited their criteria for price and location, and Rose wanted to buy the house. However, Susan was having reservations about living in it as an unmarried woman. She was a modern young lady who by graduating as an engineer had already broken some barriers encountered by women, but she had some old-fashioned ideas about a few things. The compromise was to have a civil ceremony and then in the following year have a church wedding. So, on September 25, 1981, Yvonne and I gathered with Rose's family, who resided in the Washington DC area, and Susan's mentor from General Electric at a courthouse in Maryland. We witnessed the marriage of Susan and Rose, and afterward we all got together for a nice luncheon that allowed everyone to personally congratulate the newlyweds. That night Susan moved into her new home as Mrs. Bynum.

--Susan and Rose began married life, and Yvonne and I began to make arrangements for the church wedding and reception. Our plans were to arrange for a date in early June, but somehow Mother Nature had a different intention. When Susan came home for Christmas, she announced she was pregnant. We now had two choices: have Susan walk down the aisle in the full bloom of motherhood or move up the date. The latter option seemed the most sensible, so we settled on a March church wedding, hoping that the Syracuse weather would cooperate. It half obliged us on March 20 by raining and not snowing. Few people knew about Susan's condition, and everything proceeded like a conventional wedding. It was a wonderful day, and all the guests have fond memories of celebrating Susan's church wedding—but as you might expect, Susan and Rose celebrate the September ceremony as their anniversary date.

Throughout the day I felt a sense of pride that my daughter was capable of looking beyond any racial bias in selecting her husband and also that she wanted to demonstrate a full commitment to him before living together. At the time, both these ways of thinking were not very common. I thought this stance not only favorably reflected on her, but also Yvonne and me as parents.

It should be noted that, except for a few minor incidents, our early concerns seemed unwarranted. Throughout their marriage Susan has continued her career with General Electric, while Rose has established himself as a valuable contributor for IBM. Their home life revolved around raising two sons and a daughter, who have now all completed college. Turning our parental concern into encouragement and cooperation has made us proud parents.

Larry

We were living in Munich and getting ready to go out and celebrate our anniversary when my son Larry called us from New Jersey. He wanted to offer us his congratulations, but his real reason for calling was to announce that he was planning to get married the next year on our anniversary. His fiancée Blair's parents also celebrate the same date, so they decided they would continue making it a time to remember. I was looking forward to the unstressed role of the male parent at the wedding when Larry gave us the rest of his reason for calling. He wanted to do something different for his wedding and get married in Piedmont, Italy, near the birthplace of Yvonne's parents. He had lived there for six months as a child, and then visited for two weeks as a teenager and for a short time after finishing college. We were surprised, but delighted that we could be a part of his romantic idea.

Our plan was to stay a few extra days in late October to collect information when we went to pick up my mother-in-law, Ines, for her winter visit with us. We would share our findings with Larry and Blair when we returned to the United States at Christmas. We were aware of some of the choices for having a reception and churches for the wedding, and we were hoping friends in the area would also have some suggestions.

We knew about a lovely restaurant on Lago Serio and were told about another place in a nearby town. After we collected information about these places, several people told us about a charming, typical Piedmontese restaurant just north of Ivrea. We set off on a foggy day to find the place. On the main road, which goes through the town of Settimo Vittone, is a sign that directs you to a winding road that leads to the Pra Giuli Restaurant, our destination. After a short time, the houses along the winding road disappeared, and another sign pointed to an even narrower winding road. We climbed through the fog and after driving up over 2000 feet arrived at the Pra Giuli. The place is a charming, somewhat rustic restaurant run by a husband and wife who immediately captivated Yvonne with descriptions of what they could prepare for us. As we departed, I expressed my concern about the road we had to drive on getting there. The owner was amused and laughed, and then said he drove it twice a day to take his daughter back and forth to school. After we left, I pointed out to Yvonne that navigating the road after eating and drinking all afternoon might place some unwanted stress on the guests.

To find a church, we visited the bishop in the area, and he was very helpful. We were directed to another winding roadway that led to a small chapel on the outskirts of Ivrea, and once we entered it we knew this was just the church we had hoped to find. It had only about ten rows of pews and an equal area devoted to the altar and statues of several saints. Frescoes and paintings led up to the dome, where light entered the church and cast a flattering illumination on all the artwork.

When we returned home at Christmas, we presented all our findings to Blair and Larry. As you might have guessed, they wanted the mountaintop restaurant for their reception. When I pointed out the problem it presented, Larry said there was a simple solution—hire a bus to take everyone from the church. I must admit it was a good idea, and we added this chore to our list of things to arrange.

When we brought Ines back to Vestigne in the spring, we set aside a few days to finalize the arrangements. I picked a nice clear day to drive up the mountain and actually enjoyed the journey. Unfortunately, Yvonne didn't feel the same way, but when she was most uncomfortable she just closed her eyes. The owner was delighted that we returned since it gave him the opportunity to entertain our American guests with his Piedmont cuisine. He and Yvonne spent considerable time coming up with a wonderful menu; and like a typical Italian feast, it would take a whole afternoon of eating to consume it. Between family, relatives, and friends, we were expecting about thirty-five people to attend.

The day of the wedding was sunny and quite hot, and the church attendance was swelled by people from Vestigne who wanted to see the Americans get married. The priest leading the wedding ceremony and the renewal of vows by Yvonne and me and Blair's parents was Father Primo, Ines's cousin, who spoke no English. From the time Blair walked down the aisle with her father until we all gathered for pictures in the church courtyard, everything went along smoothly. Larry told me later the part that brought tears to his eyes was hearing his parents renew their vows. We cherished being a part of his wedding.

Sitting in the bus for my third trip up the mountain was most enjoyable; and as we climbed, the day became cooler. When we reached the parking lot, the refreshing breezes and the spectacular view of the valley below made it apparent that our selection of the Pra Guili was an excellent decision. This became even more apparent when we finished eating the spectacular dinner, which demonstrated the variety and sophistication of the Piedmont cuisine. That evening everyone, along with some village people, gathered at a tennis club near Vestigne to relax at a party given by Ines. She wanted to do her bit to make the day memorable.

Like Susan and Rose, Blair and Larry bought a house after getting engaged. Larry lived in it for six months prior to getting married, and it was the site of a party they gave for family and friends in the United States when they returned as husband and wife. The affair was a rousing success and was a fitting way to end the wedding celebration.

The only glitch in their wedding was that Blair and Larry had to wait almost a year before Italian authorities sent them the paperwork that established the legality of their marriage. The day of the ceremony was an international event since three American couples had recited wedding vows in response to a priest speaking Italian. Although most Ivreans didn't notice, many of those in attendance that day will never forget the occasion. It made Ivrea a special place for many of us.

Yvonne and I were most pleased by the fact that our son wanted to connect with our past and make us such an important part of his wedding. As parents, you are always full of pride when your children show their love for you.

Today Blair and Larry are the proud parents of three lovely young ladies.

Ray

Our youngest was the last to get married. He met Tia when he was thirty-four, and after a short time of dating he moved in with her. Tia was an engineer working for a local power company in Kansas City and was able to buy her own house, so living together made them appear like any newly married couple. It seemed they were committed to each other, but there was no talk about a wedding. However, we treated them like a married couple. We visited them at Tia's house and went on vacations with them. On a trip to Breckenridge, Colorado, we were joined by Tia's parents, Shirley and Leonard Johnsen, and it turned out to be a very nice family gathering. At that time,

Ray began to experience the first signs of an illness that would plague him for several years. He went through a series of tests and examinations that never revealed his problem, so it was assumed that he had chronic fatigue syndrome. It's an Illness that constantly leaves you feeling in a weakened condition. For a time he was able to work only half a day, and getting married seemed to be a difficult step to take. However, the support and understanding that Tia gave him never wavered and helped him immensely in coping with his illness. We treated her as a member of the family and were grateful for the aid she gave him, and we hoped that one day they would be married.

Ray began to feel better, and he and Tia planned a vacation with the Johnsens and Yvonne and me at a unique place called Mackinac Island, located in Michigan on the waters of Lake Huron. It can be reached by a short boat ride from Mackinaw City; and when you arrive, transportation is limited to walking or using horse-drawn carriages, bicycles, or saddle horses. We had brought our bikes since our accommodations were located away from the docking area. We spent our first day riding around on our bicycles acquainting ourselves with our surroundings. Since the island is only three miles long and two miles wide, this was not a difficult undertaking. However, that evening we were all a little tired and retired early.

The next morning, we heard a knock on the door. When I opened it, there was Tia attired in a long white dress with a veil on her head, and Ray was wearing dark pants with a nice patterned vest and a white shirt. They said, "We want to invite you to our wedding today." We were flabbergasted, but we soon recovered and then gave them warm embraces to show our joy. They then knocked on the Johnsens' door next door to our room. When they saw the scene in the hall and heard the news, their expressions showed the same shock we must have shown. We were told to get dressed and come down to the horse-drawn carriage waiting for us. None of us had brought clothing suitable for a wedding. The women managed to dress in clothes that looked quite presentable, but Leonard and I had on attire that belonged on a golf course.

When we appeared downstairs, there were two chauffeured carriages waiting: one for Tia, Ray, and the preacher, and the other for the parents. We rode to a bluff overlooking the water, and our small group assembled to give the wedding couple a splendid view of the vista while the ceremony was taking place. It was a short service, but the smiles on all our faces showed the ritual was especially pleasing and an exceptional way to start a marriage. We were then driven into town and were dropped off at a marina where there was a boat waiting for us. It seems our children were going to treat us to a boat ride around the island. We now had time to discuss our surprise about the events taking place. Shirley was especially shocked because she had talked with and seen her daughter quite frequently, but she had no inkling about the occasion. It was obvious that Tia and Ray both enjoyed all the planning they went through and the surprise they had subjected us to.

When we returned from our boat ride, Tia and Ray figured that they had to feed us, and had made reservations at the Grand Hotel a short distance from the town. The place has an international reputation, and several years before it was made the focal point of a movie starring Christopher Reeve. It is a historic resort on beautiful landscaped grounds overlooking the Straits of Mackinac. We were served a wonderful breakfast, and we thanked the newlyweds for the spectacular day they had given us. In fact, it was an unforgettable day.

We were especially full of pride that Ray needed to only share his wedding with us to make it a memorable event for him. During his years of illness and courtship, Ray, through phone calls and occasional visits, always made us feel that our encouragement and backing were important to his future happiness.

At Christmas that year we hosted a large party to proudly introduce the newlyweds to our Syracuse friends.

Like his sister and brother, Ray has also made us proud grandparents of three offspring, three energetic and spirited boys.

Our children are spread across the country, from New Jersey to Kansas and California, so for holidays and major events we find ourselves driving or flying to see them. We envy people who have their children living nearby, but weekly phone calls help bridge the gap into their daily lives. Each of them started out their marriages differently, but they have contributed to making all of us one big happy family.

Celebrating a Fiftieth Wedding Anniversary

Our three children made such a wonderful effort to make the event exceptional and memorable.

Being married to each other for over fifty years is certainly an accomplishment my wife and I are both quite proud of. I know many in our current society marvel at such an achievement, but friends in our generation seem quite often to have reached this landmark in their life. It requires that love evolve into a state of compatibility, where one's faults are tolerated and sharing similar desires and ideas fosters a zest for life. Of course, it also requires being in good health, a fact that prevented my parents from achieving this milestone. Nowadays a factor limiting this attainment is that people are getting married later in life. I was only twenty-five and my wife was twenty when we entered the state of matrimony. So you see, a lot of fortunate things occurred to have us reach our fiftieth anniversary.

The thing that made the occasion most auspicious was that we had three children to help celebrate it with us. All families who realize this type of achievement do something to commemorate the occasion, but we were lucky that our children were so clever and thoughtful about making the event memorable.

They focused our attention on assembling all our Syracuse friends together for feasting at an extravagant barbecue in the picturesque Jamesville County Park. They sent out invitations to our Syracuse friends and selected the weekend following the actual anniversary date for the picnic. They gave us some plausible reason why this was a more convenient date. We were a little disappointed, because this meant we would have to celebrate the actual date by ourselves. My son, Larry, casually asked us to come down to New Jersey and take in a Broadway show with them. They celebrate their anniversary date on the same day; it seemed like a great idea, and we readily accepted the invitation.

We arrived early on Friday afternoon at Larry and Blair's house, and the start of surprises began to occur. They gave us a gift certificate to spend at a nearby spa. Yvonne decided a manicure would be a treat for her, and I was happy to find out that I could skip the pedicure and experience a massage. We returned home to find our son Ray, Tia, and their three boys in the living room to greet us. We had been planning to meet them the next week in the Adirondacks to spend a few days together enjoying the summer mountain climate before they came to our anniversary party. The weekend was beginning to seem a little more complicated than we had anticipated.

After dinner that evening, Larry said he had an errand to do and left us for a while. He returned an hour later and walked in the door escorting our daughter, Susan. Having our three children with us on our anniversary was certainly a wonderful surprise. Larry assured us that arrangements had been made to accommodate the increase in theater patrons. Tia couldn't go with us because she had to take care of the children, especially Trent who was only nine months old. Larry and Blair had made babysitting arrangements for their three girls. Yvonne and I went to sleep that night anticipating a nice day in Manhattan with our children.

Soon after lunch a big limousine pulled into Larry's driveway. He said, "We are going to ride to the theater in style." Getting to the theater in Manhattan with six people is a bit complicated, so taking a limousine made some sense. After we were seated, Larry opened a bottle of champagne to get the celebration started. I had hoped that there wasn't much traffic because there wasn't time to spare before the matinee started. Larry didn't seem very concerned, and I began to wonder if Yvonne and I were headed for a different destination. When we passed the turnoff for the Lincoln Tunnel, I knew our children had different plans for us. As we traveled over the George Washington Bridge, I still couldn't figure where we were headed. Our children laughed and gave us all kinds of misleading hints. When we went over the Triborough Bridge into Astoria, I began to see the light. We were headed to the Mount Carmel Church where Yvonne and I were married fifty years ago.

After we parked in front of the church, Blair opened a box that she had brought in the car and unveiled a bouquet of artificial flowers that were almost an exact replica of the ones Yvonne carried down the aisle on our wedding day. Blair had created this marvelous gift after studying pictures in our wedding album. Yvonne was close to tears as she cradled the flowers in her arms. Of course, they also had a flower for me to pin on my lapel. We were told to enter the church; and as we walked down the aisle, we noticed a priest waiting at the altar for us. As we got close, we also noticed our good friend, Marie Roberts, who stood in this same church fifty years ago, welcoming us as she was doing this day.

The priest explained he was going to conduct a brief wedding mass and was going to ask us to renew our vows. After so many years, the ceremony has a different significance. The first time, I am sure everyone must wonder a little how long the state of wedded bliss will last. After fifty years, you know you made the correct choice and did something right with your marriage and are now reminded that you have successfully carried out your vows. After the ceremony, our children and Marie congratulated us and we were led back to the limo waiting for us outside the church.

It was too late for the theater, but we headed to Manhattan across the Fifty-Ninth Street Bridge and soon found ourselves on Central Park South, a street filled with many fancy hotels. Our wedding night was spent at such a hotel, called the San Moritz. We stopped in front of a hotel called the Ritz Carlton, which we soon found out was the luxuriously renovated San Moritz. It was good to know that our marriage had outlived the life of our wedding-night hotel. Larry and Blair took our suitcase, which Blair had hastily repacked and which they had earlier slipped into the trunk of the limo, and told us to go inside and register for the night. They were all doing such a wonderful job of recreating our wedding day. The room we were directed to was a far cry from the small, non-air-conditioned place we spent our first night as husband and wife. We were requested not to spend too much time getting comfortable since there was more we had to do.

When we got downstairs, the limo had left and we were told we were going for a walk. We strolled downtown for a couple of blocks, and shortly found ourselves in front of the Warwick Hotel. The cycle was now complete, because this was where our wedding reception dinner was hosted. We entered the lounge, and after a round of cocktails was served, we all shared the excitement of our day together. Yvonne could not stop showing the pleasure that came from all the surprises she had experienced.

The hotel didn't have a restaurant open to the public, so we were going to have dinner at a nearby place that Larry knew about. Before going, Yvonne and I wanted to find the banquet room where our reception had been held. I had seen it for only a couple hours on our wedding day, but Yvonne had made the arrangements, so she was more familiar with the hotel. When we finally found the room, my memory bank was stimulated into recalling the friends and family that had gathered to celebrate. I especially remembered my mother (who had recently recovered from serious brain surgery) enjoying herself so much. Yvonne's mother, who had left most of the planning to her daughter, seemed relieved and happy that day that her only child had arranged such an elegant affair for her relatives and friends.

After a second round of drinks, we decided it was time to walk to the nearby restaurant where Larry had made reservations. It was a wonderful dinner that took several hours to consume. We were escorted back to the Ritz Carlton and then we parted company. Enjoying the luxury of our room was a real treat, and we took our time preparing to retire for the evening. Our preparations were interrupted by a knock at the door, announcing that room service had been ordered. A cart containing a bottle of champagne and two domed dishes of food was pushed into the room. We raised the domes; one revealed a plate of French fries, while under the other dome we discovered two tuna fish sandwiches. It took us awhile to realize that our children had remembered that the night after our reception dinner we got hungry and snacked on tuna fish sandwiches. Having our children remember such a small detail brought tears to our eyes. It shows how important little things can be in making an impression. Our children had really given us a memorable day of wonderful, thoughtful surprises.

The following week's celebration was quite different. Yvonne and I arrived at the park on a beautiful summer day. Our Syracuse friends and our whole family, who numbered over fifty people, were gathered about a large covered shelter awaiting our arrival. Our children had taken several pictures from our wedding album and blown them up to almost life size and hung them from the shelter's roof. We were reminded all day how fifty years had changed us, a fate we shared with our friends.

One of the highlights of the day was when everyone gathered for a group picture. The photographer had a panoramic camera that allowed him to make a picture where everyone was recognizable. It hangs in our home as a reminder of how many people we have shared our lives with.

Beer and wine put everyone in a festive mood, and the delicious barbecue put on by the Dinosaur Restaurant more than satisfied the crowd's appetite.

When it came time for me to say something, I revealed to everyone the details of our special day from the previous week.

Yvonne and I mixed in with all our guests and enjoyed all the congratulations about our marriage and our wonderful family. It was another day when we were made to realize how fortunate we were.

GETTING OLD

*In recent years I began to notice my aging, and I
felt obliged to write about the process.*

Every day we confront the subject of aging, but we seldom think of it as getting old. Becoming older means we are maturing, gaining in experience, or becoming worldlier—not that we are old. This condition is something we avoid by ignoring it or by trying many remedies that mask it or make us overlook the state. I am at an age where I can no longer fool myself or ignore the situation and I look back wondering how I got where I am.

As a young person I participated in many team sports. Once I finished college and got married, all that physical activity ceased and I spent my time working, raising three children, and going to school at night. I had put on a few pounds, but only my wife really noticed. A professional athlete in his early thirties would detect he had slowed down a bit and would be reminded that he was getting old. The only inkling I had of my advancing years was when I saw a few gray hairs appear and when young people started to address me as "sir." When my children were in their preteen years, I started to get active again and took up tennis and skiing. I briefly tried my hand at golf, but found I didn't play too well and gave it up. Tennis was a sport where my aggressiveness paid off, and I managed to be competitive as long as I played people close to my age or those who had limited playing experience. An hour or two of some spirited competition gave me enough exercise to make my body sweat and ache, and reminded me of how I felt in my youth after an afternoon playing basketball in the park. I was approaching forty years of age, and I needed some assurance that my physical prowess had not diminished too drastically. My son at the age of forty had to reassure himself of a similar concern, and he took up long-distance running. By running the New York Marathon at forty, he convinced himself that he had the same physical stamina of his football-playing days. The body may be aging, but if the spirit is robust, you can fail to notice some small deterioration.

Skiing was another sport that gave me a youthful feeling. When our youngest child was six and the oldest was ten, my wife and I set out with them to test our skill and endurance on the ski slopes. As parents, we were less daring and learned at a slower rate than our children, but we did manage to reach a level of competence that gave us a great deal of satisfaction. Skiing is a great sport because it allows you to control the level of challenge you want to experience. You can go down the easier slopes or go more slowly down the more difficult hills. Our children looked for jumps to make them airborne; we were content to traverse a mogul without falling. Besides being a sport to test our physical competence, skiing was an activity to bind our family. It is hard to think of an endeavor that offers so much benefit.

Another thing that can take your mind off your advancing years is watching your children go through their teenage years and see some of the ability you may have possessed being developed in them. All three of our children were active in many team sports, and I spent a great deal of time watching, cheering them on, and in some cases, even coaching their activities. Participating in these ways led to keeping me connected with activities of my youth and showed support for my children's efforts.

Like most people that go through their forties and fifties, my wife and I had the benefit of good health. However, in these latter years, there was a small glitch that occurred in our well-being. Yvonne developed a swollen right knee and a Baker's cyst. Soon after her problem arose, I started to experience a similar discomfort in my left knee. It was almost like sleeping together passed on the condition to me! We found an orthopedic surgeon who said in most cases like ours, he could solve the problem with arthroscopic surgery. He was the physician for the Syracuse University football team, so having him operate on us made it appear like a youthful malady. The procedure was successful, and for many years we enjoyed trouble-free use of our knees.

Shortly after this temporary setback, Yvonne and I went on a ski trip to Aspen. We left on Friday evening and arrived at a hotel outside of Aspen at 2:00 a.m. After a late breakfast, we were transported to the Aspen Highlands ski area for an afternoon of skiing. Every day during the following week, we went skiing at one of the four areas near Aspen. On Sunday, the day we were to leave, a bus came by early and took us to Copper Mountain, a ski area on the way to the airport. After a full day of skiing and a late dinner, we boarded a red-eye flight and arrived in Syracuse at 6:00 a.m. It was quite a hectic week, and Yvonne and I rejoiced that we had the stamina and physical ability to not only survive our adventure, but to also enjoy it—something only a youthful person obviously could do.

Looking in a mirror over the years, I couldn't help noticing the change taking place. My hair was getting grayer and it was thinning out, but my wife kept telling me I looked cute, so the aging process never concerned me too much. For a short time, I did resort to putting some coloring in my hair; but Yvonne said the graying gave me a distinguished look, so I stopped.

In my late fifties I went to work in Germany for four years, working hard in a demanding and satisfying job as the technical director of a four-nation consortium, traveling all over Europe and participating for exercise in skiing, volksmarches, biking, and tennis. It was a good life and an exciting one. After four years we decided it was time to return home; and since I was approaching sixty-two years old, I felt it was time also to experience the world of a retiree. During my later years with the company, I saw many people sort of retire on the job. They had lost their ambition and enthusiasm, attributes that earlier contributed to their professional performance and satisfaction. Ending my career by successfully handling my most challenging responsibility gave me a young-at-heart feeling about myself. I knew General Electric would not be able to offer me a position that would compare to the satisfaction I obtained from my European assignment, so retirement was an attractive option.

Retirement offers one the opportunity to change many aspects of your life and take it in a different direction. During my many years of skiing out west, I became enamored with the idea of living like a ski bum for a while. To me, this meant being concerned each day only with taking care of our very basic necessities and deciding where we were going to pass the time skiing. Putting your skis on fresh-fallen snow, soaking up the warmth of a bright sunny day, and pushing your body to carve sweeping turns down a challenging hill always seemed like an exhilarating way to spend your time. Places that provided such an uplifting experience for me were the six expert trails on the back side of Northstar Mountain at Lake Tahoe. Over a mile of skiing steep, varying pitched slopes without stopping left your thighs aching and your lungs gasping for air, but I felt so great on the way up the lift. For three years, Yvonne and I lived a skier's dream by spending the month of March enjoying the wonderful resorts at the north end of the lake, but slowly our knees began to feel the strain our lifestyle was exacting. In the future we limited our activities to skiing locally and short trips out west. We made another concession to our advancing years and had a doctor prescribe braces for our ailing knees. Since our ski pants covered the contraptions, no one knew we needed assistance. It was a small price to pay for being able to continue to ski.

When I retired, I continued to play tennis for several years, but my body rebelled against the stress it put on knees and back. I tried using my knee brace and a back brace while playing tennis, and while these devices may have solicited some sympathy when I played, they didn't help relieve much of the discomfort. It was obvious that my joints were getting more arthritic; and after a couple of years of enduring the pain, I decided to make another adaption to my advancing years and gave up playing tennis. It was a very disappointing step to take, and I tried to compensate for the setback by taking up golf again. I never reached the same level of satisfaction with this game, but it did get me out in the good weather and, at times, led to moments of pleasure. After all, even a mediocre golfer gets lucky once in awhile and hits a shot that would make a pro happy.

I found that swimming was a good exercise for my ailing joints. I swam at the high school pool during the winter and at the town pool in the summer. I was really trying to keep in shape. At that time in my life, I felt I had slowed down a bit, but I didn't feel old and my waistline still allowed me to wear size 36 pants. I continued to perform all the basic chores around the house, went to the gym three times a week, and looked forward to skiing and taking trips each winter. Our friends had differing experiences with the aging process, and the subject was always a favorite topic of conversation. These discussions often made me feel better because it showed that many of my friends had more to complain about, but I became fond of going out with younger people because health issues seldom came up for discussion.

One thing all in my age group had in common was the strange way our minds began to work. We could walk into another room and then wonder why we were there, or the name of something we knew really well would not connect with our consciousness. I was told that the brain has difficulty making connections with the memory bank as you get older. On the other hand, I am often amazed at some of the things I remember as I do a crossword puzzle. Also, fortunately, many memories of my past are quite vivid, and recalling these recollections with my wife is a way of making them a part of our present life. An advantage of aging is that it gives us more remembrances to share.

During the years after my retirement, I made several trips to Europe for business and pleasure. I hadn't lost the zest for adventure, and I had my mother-in-law as a role model. She stayed with Yvonne and me from October through March and returned to her home in Italy for the rest of the year. She started this practice after her husband died when she was seventy-one, and continued to travel back and forth until she was ninety-seven. Her feistiness and passion for life were catching, and I always marveled at her attitude. She seldom complained about her physical condition and disliked when a doctor or anyone considered her old. She made me realize how much your mental outlook affects your perception of aging. I was determined that I wouldn't start to feel sorry for myself.

When I was seventy-one, I had an accident that seriously hampered my physical activities. I slipped on the ice and broke the femur bone in my left leg. It happened in February and ruined most of the ski season for me. The misfortune slowed me down for a while, but that spring I was back on the golf course and the following winter I returned to the ski slopes. But it was obvious that the knees of both Yvonne and me were a problem and at times caused us both a lot of discomfort. Tylenol gave us frequent temporary relief. We continued to use the medication to maintain our active lifestyle, but it was becoming more difficult. One day, during a visit to a local ski area when I was seventy-seven and Yvonne seventy-two, we had an unpleasant time on the slopes, and it made us question our resolve to continue skiing. After only a half-hour of skiing, the pain in Yvonne's knee made her quit and go into the lodge. I continued to ski, but I fell twice on one run while trying to keep the stress off my knee. Afterward in the lodge, we decided that we should give our knees a break and stop skiing. It was a sad day for us. We had both been to an orthopedic surgeon and he was ready to give us new knees, but neither of us was ready to take that drastic step.

The discomfort we felt was aggravated by the house we lived in. It was a colonial, with four bedrooms on the second floor and a basement that contained the washer, dryer, a pantry, and a workshop. Going up and down the stairs several times during the day was a common occurrence, so we were constantly reminded about our problem. We finally decided that a ranch-type house would help greatly in relieving the pain we felt at times. We contracted with a builder putting up homes near where we lived and looked forward to a rather major, but welcome, change in our lifestyle.

Just prior to moving to our new house, my recently developing clumsiness caused me to have another serious accident. I stepped off the deck being built at our new house, thinking it was a short distance from the ground; the actual two-foot height caused my right knee to buckle under me, tearing the tendons around my knee. It was a painful incident and required extensive surgery to fix the problem. I couldn't bend my knee for eight weeks, and it required several weeks of physical therapy to regain a reasonably pain-free use of the leg. I now had two legs with questionable reliability, and it began to affect my balance and confidence in walking over uneven terrain and going up and down stairs. I now began to feel like I was getting old.

The doctors I visited to examine some of my minor complaints always told me I looked much younger than my age and that I had no serious health issues, but they all added comments or specified treatment that made me somewhat dispirited. My general practitioner started me on hypertension and cholesterol medication. The urologist decided I needed to begin taking Flomax. The eye, ear, and nose doctor said my occasional vertigo was caused by a loss of liquid in my inner ear, which occurs in someone of my age. The ophthalmologist said my double vision often occurs in elderly people. The audiologist said my hearing was degrading, which is common in an older person, and I would soon be a candidate for a hearing aid. The cardiologist said the atrial fibrillation that I experienced often occurs in someone of my age. Age was always the common factor that explained my conditions. It is no wonder I now felt I was old. I was glad I had a first-rate health insurance policy. This feeling of getting old would disappear after my doctors' visits, but I noticed I became more cautious as I moved about.

There is sometimes a tendency to give in to the sense of being over the hill. I have seen friends who have aged beyond their physical limitations by trying to avoid all departures from their daily routines, and they become stressed and tired when forced to make changes. Sometimes it seems like they enjoy getting old and the attention they receive when people help them cope. Avoiding stress can make for a tranquil life; but without some stress, one's existence can get to be boring. Building a new house and selling our old one certainly caused my wife and me a bit of anxiety, but it was also exciting and led to a brand-new outlook on our well-being. The newness of so many things was refreshing, and the openness of the house made us more aware of the outdoors; also, the reduction of trauma on our knees by not having to climb stairs was a welcome modification to our daily activities.

Being old in our culture is not revered as it was in the past; the rapid change in technology makes the elderly at times look outdated and somewhat retarded. However, I realize that familiarity with the latest technology is not like wisdom or knowledge, which are qualities that can bring fulfillment to your existence. So in spite of the changes taking place in my life, I feel good about myself. I have three children and nine grandchildren whose successful lives I can share, a wife who is a comfort and assists me in coping with each day, and the financial security to maintain our modest lifestyle. I feel I have accepted the challenges and recognize the benefits of aging, so it is easier to cope with getting old—but complaining at times helps relieve some of the frustration.

THE LAST HURRAH

*We continue our Italian travel adventures with probably
our last trip to Piedmont, a place that is special for us.*

During my life I have made many visits to Italy, most times accompanied by
my wife. We have been to places frequented by tourists—like Rome, Florence,
and Venice, and locations that see few American tourists—like the Cinque
Terre, the Gargano, and Urbino. We went by boat to Palermo and circled
Sicily and traveled up the Almafi Drive; all these places and many others I
have written about in my book *Sharing a Lifetime Passion for Europe*. However,
over the years we have developed a special connection with the province
of Piedmont, the town of Ivrea, and the village of Vestigne, places where
Yvonne's parents were born and raised. The link occurred from our many trips
to the area and countless visits with relatives and friends of Yvonne's parents.
During the time between stays, Yvonne maintains a connection with some of
the people through periodic phone calls. So you can see we have established
a special attachment for the place, which I wrote about in my book *Bonding
with Piedmont*. Over the later years of my life, this area has become very
familiar and significant to me.

Since we left five years ago in 2004, Yvonne has maintained through
her phone calls frequent contact with her cousin Franco and his sister Irma.
Franco is ninety-three, and Irma is ninety-eight years old. Both are in good
health, and except for Irma's bad hip causing her to use a walker, they hardly
show their age. When Yvonne talks to them, they usually ask, "Will we ever
see you again?" She is made to feel guilty when she offers no answer. Yvonne
had approached me with the idea of returning on several occasions, but my
enthusiasm never equaled her own; but I realized I would be even less likely
to embrace the idea as I get older. When we travel in Italy we are on our own,
and the experience is a lot different than being led around by a tour guide.

So, before my age becomes too much of a convenient excuse, I decided I had enough interest in seeing Italy one more time and the confidence to adapt to the cultural changes.

Long before we decided to go, Yvonne's cousin, Angelo Fornero, had offered his unoccupied family home in the village of Vestigne for us to use. On our last trip five years ago, we stayed at an unoccupied apartment in the town of Ivrea. It was owned by the daughter of a good neighbor of Yvonne's mother in the village. You can see how welcome we are made to feel. We accepted Angelo's generous hospitality and made plane and car reservations for a two-week visit. The only definite plan we made before leaving was to celebrate Yvonne's birthday by reserving a room for two nights on Lago di Garda, Italy's largest lake. It was a place we had visited years before with my brother and his wife.

The basic intent in going to Italy was to experience, probably for the last time, doing the little things we had enjoyed doing before and that gave us comfort and fond memories. Then, of course, there was the desire to see people we had gotten to know over the years and who had been so kind to us. What we didn't realize was that having these experiences during our visit meant living a little like an Italian and not like an American tourist.

Our journey began by driving to New Jersey on Wednesday and having Larry take us to the Newark Airport. Our first problem on arriving in Italy early Thursday morning was trying to get out of the confusing roads in the rental car parking lot; but after seeing our dilemma, a nice attendant walked over to show us the exit that freed us from the maze. I was soon on familiar roads and found our way to Vestigne, where Angelo and his wife Maria Teresa were waiting at their family house. After Angelo gave me a lesson on how to navigate my car down a narrow street and park it in his gated driveway, he proceeded to show us the house. I found out later it had been built in the seventeenth century and his family had owned the place for three generations.

It was a large home comprising three floors, and we were told there were two options for using it during our stay. On the third floor was an apartment with a small kitchen and an eating area, a living room where we could watch the BBC on TV, and two bedrooms and a bathroom with a small tub and a hand shower. The other choice was to occupy a large bedroom with a bath on the second floor, and use the kitchen, eating area, and living room on the first floor, which also contained a large modern bathroom with a walk-in shower. We actually wound up living on the third floor in the early morning and late evening and on the first floor during the rest of the day. We always made sure we left nothing we needed behind as we traversed the stairs each day.

The inside of the house showed none of its age. It was furnished with traditional Italian pieces, and the walls were covered with interesting paintings. Each floor had a balcony that looked out on a big patio that contained two large awnings to provide shade during the hot afternoons. The opposite side of the patio was bordered by two buildings that in years past contained farm animals and equipment. Now they housed an extra car and some wine-making gear. The basement below the building was where Angelo has his wine cellar. His stock was so large he could skip making wine for a few years, but the tradition of making wine each year was an old one that Angelo could not ignore.

It is interesting to note that every door in the house had a key for maintaining security. Each day we had to use different keys for our upstairs apartment, the stairwell, the door to the downstairs rooms, and the iron gate leading to the driveway. I was always afraid I might lose a key or lock myself out of a room.

After we were escorted throughout the house, Maria Teresa put a delicious dinner for us on the table. She had a variety of sliced meats for antipasti bought from the store across the street, and from home she brought roast chicken with mashed potatoes and a tasty caponata for a vegetable. She offered cheese and fruit to finish the meal, but we were too full to indulge.

After eating, they insisted that we take a nap to help overcome our jet lag. While we slept, Angelo bottled some of his wine from last year and his wife cleaned up. After we woke up, we continued to fill each other in on events and showed them pictures of our family that we brought with us. Angelo speaks some English, and I feel comfortable talking with him. I noticed a distinct improvement in his communication by the time we left.

Our hosts were in no hurry to return to their house outside Turin, and before we knew it, it was time to eat supper. Maria Teresa brought out a salad that she dressed with an oil and vinegar dressing seasoned with tuna fish, which gave it a special flavor. The cheese platter, which contained the creamiest, most delicious Gorgonzola I ever tasted, was attacked with vigor. Our first day was certainly filled with an abundance of what Italy is noted for: good food. The leftovers were put in the refrigerator for us.

On Friday morning we tried to use the small tub with a hand shower to wash, but found it to be an awkward undertaking and decided we would take our showers downstairs. Later, the Forneros informed us that they had invited Irma and Franco to join us for a feast on Saturday in Vestigue. We told them we would augment the dishes for the meal. So after saying hello to some of Yvonne's mother's neighbors, we set out for Carrefour's, a Wal-Mart-type store in Ivrea, except the food section is so much more interesting. We bought prosciutto and other sliced meats, ravioli, and what turned out to be a delicious porcini mushroom sauce, sardines, and anchovies. The fennel looked so tender we decided to sauté them with some garlic for a vegetable. We were satisfied with our purchases, but were disappointed that, after searching throughout Ivrea, we could find no English-language newspaper as we had years before. To complete our contribution to the meal, on the way home we purchased a tray of the popular Italian pastries.

The next day Angelo and his wife arrived before noon, bringing Irma and food from home with them. Irma moved slowly with her walker, but her face and attire made her look so much younger than her actual years; when she spoke to Yvonne, her speech was strong and enthusiastic. Her brother, who had driven by himself to Vestigne, arrived shortly after her, looking just like I remembered him from five years earlier. He was nicely dressed and carrying his contribution to the meal, a box of the traditional Italian pastries. If you think Italians are preoccupied with food, you are probably right, but eating was one of the highlights of our trip because their cuisine is so important to them.

While Yvonne and Maria Teresa were assembling and preparing all the dishes in the kitchen, the rest of us were outside drinking Angelo's wine and enjoying the pleasantly warm day. The dining table had been set up on a large miller's stone that sat on a pedestal in the patio. The array of antipasti that were brought out was so appealing. There were two types of cold sliced meats followed by the sardines and the anchovies we had brought. Maria Teresa showed off her cooking skill by making pancakes from the mashed potatoes left over from the day of our arrival. Then she spread over large slices of fresh tomatoes and chicken breasts some of her homemade mayonnaise seasoned with tuna fish. Finally, she had taken from home several large sage leaves and prepared them for the table by first dipping them in sparkling water, then flour, and frying them in oil. As you bit into the crunchy bubbles of coating, the mild taste of the fresh sage was enhanced. After sampling all these offerings along with some bread or grissini, your appetite began to wane a little. However, everyone still had a desire for the next course, which consisted of ravioli with porcini sauce. No one wanted to tackle the main course of roast veal, sautéed fennel, and Swiss chard. After all, one had to leave some appetite for the pastries. Maria Teresa took the main-course dishes home with her.

Instead of a siesta, Yvonne and I went with Franco and Irma to the village cemetery, where several relatives are buried. Irma never left the parked car, but I think she may have thought being so close made her prayers more effective. Italians frequently go to the cemetery and many of the burial sites are filled with fresh flowers and plants, making a colorful complement to the gray vaults and tombstones. During our stay we visited five cemeteries; we said prayers for Yvonne's parents in Ivrea, her cousin Luciano in Albiano, Franco's wife, Ines, in Robbio, and Felice, a good friend's husband, in Borgomasino. It has been somewhat of a tradition with Yvonne and me because we did the same thing during our last visit. The people we prayed for were all ones with whom we had had close relationships.

On Sunday we had a day of rest from extravagant eating and visited Mari, Luciano's wife, who had spent years comforting her husband as he tried coping with the discomforts caused by a stroke. Since his passing away, she has become a frequent traveler outside of Italy and she took pride in sharing pictures of all her trips. After visiting the cemetery together, we drove to nearby Piverone Lake and shared ice cream and soft drinks together while observing all the Italians enjoying a beautiful Sunday afternoon. Mari's life had improved so much since her husband died, she sometimes felt guilty about it. Yvonne repeatedly tried to ease her conscience by telling her she earned the good fortune she was now enjoying.

That night I ate a tasty pizza in the little trattoria a block from where we were staying, while Yvonne ate a flavorsome fish caught at the lake we had visited that afternoon. The meal demonstrated what I had been told: there is no such thing as a bad place to eat in Italy.

The day we left for Lago di Garda, the rains came to Piedmont and the drive to the Hotel Gardesana in Torri di Benaco was not too pleasant. We made the trip with only a few minor wrong turns, but I found that driving in Italy had changed since five years earlier. Now almost every intersection had a circle to control the traffic flow. As you enter one, a sign shows you the exits from the rotunda with the names of towns that you will eventually come to. You should know all towns on your route because your destination might not appear until you get close. The names are clearly marked, but sometimes the one you are looking for will disappear from the signs and then you must try and follow what appears to be the main road. Most routes are numbered and you will see signs marking the road, but except for the numbers of the autostradas or major toll highways, the lesser roads are not indicated on the rotundas. You never get sleepy driving because you must pay such close attention. I never felt embarrassed when I had to go around a circle for the second time.

The hotel where we were going to stay for two nights lies at the south end of a pedestrian-only area; and its rooms, a dining balcony, and a large outdoor café face a small horseshoe-shaped marina leading directly to the lake. It's a picturesque scene that tourists admire while sipping a drink or simply strolling about. On our last visit we took a couple of pictures that now hang on the wall of our home. They are constant reminders of the serenity and simple things that make Italy so delightful.

The rain had stopped, and after checking in we joined the promenade and triggered our memories from over ten years earlier. When we returned, I asked the desk clerk what time dinner was served. He said, "The restaurant opens at seven, but Italians don't eat until eight." Being Italians, we arrived at the appointed time and found the place completely occupied. It was then that we realized the town is not filled with Italians, but Germans. The waiter sat us at a table in the bar and brought us glasses of refreshing Prosecco, which made the short wait a relaxing respite. The meal was excellent. My appetizer was three different smoked fish and salad, followed by an entrée of a veal chop with eggplant. Yvonne had carpaccio, and she said the scallops were delicious. By the time we were finished eating, all the German patrons had left and then we noticed some Italian tourists.

The next day the rain clouds had disappeared and the sun teased us with its warmth. After one of those big breakfasts that German tourists require, we strolled among the shops looking, but not buying, except for a copy of *USA Today*. Later, with our paper and our books, we found a comfortable place to read and watch the whitecaps on the lake. We had decided that a gelato and a peach were enough food until supper.

That night we had dinner at the sparsely patronized restaurant on the second floor of the hotel. With so few diners, the waiter had time to regale us with the 500-year history of the hotel and all the celebrity visitors that they had hosted. He talked me into drinking a glass of very fine Bardolino wine, which I found out later cost $20. It was expensive, but it was quite good.

The next day the rains returned, and our drive back to Vestigne was in poor visibility and hard downpours. It was a little stressful since many Italian drivers don't slow down in bad weather. The day after our return, we visited Cesare and Mariuccia Angera in Ivrea. They have four children, three of whom work in the paint factory they own. Nowadays they spend a lot of their time babysitting their grandchildren. The day we saw them, Mariuccia was helping their cute eleven-month-old blond, blue-eyed grandson to walk. With six grandchildren, another on the way, a live-in sister, and nearby brother and wife, family gatherings require a good deal of space; fortunately their apartment is spacious. A few days later when we visited Mariuccia's brother, Renzo, and his wife, Maria Teresa, the same blond, blue-eyed baby was at their house. The child gets the tender loving care of the grandparents or the aunt and uncle each day of the week as the mother is working. You could tell that Maria Teresa, who couldn't have children, enjoyed her role as a caregiver. As she lovingly cradled the fussing baby to her ample bosom in comforting him, she commented to Yvonne that she never thought at her age she would have the pleasure of minding a baby.

Their home is really a villa, with hot water pipes in the floor for heating and a beautiful balustrade made by Renzo, which guides you between the marbled floors. Several doors lead you to patios that are surrounded by flower boxes and outdoor furniture, where you can view their large vegetable garden. Living only a block from his sister, Renzo and his wife are affectionately embraced by the large Angera family. Visiting each family makes us aware of how much Italians revere their kin, and each time we see them, they enthusiastically welcome us.

The weekend after our return from Lago di Garda, the Forneros planned on spending their time with us. We started out on Friday by meeting them on the way to visiting the hilltop town of Montiglio in the Asti province. I had read about the place on the Internet, and I was glad that Angelo was driving because I would have had great difficulty in finding the place.

We arrived at lunchtime, and since Italians have light breakfasts, I knew they were hungry, so I suggested first stopping to eat before we went touring. I wanted to treat them to lunch to partially repay them for the hospitality they had been showing us. I asked Angelo to inquire about a suitable restaurant. He was told about the Cascina Rosengana, an agriturismo in the neighboring hilltop town of Cocconato. An agriturismo is a farmhouse that has been refashioned to offer food and sometimes lodging for tourists. They are very popular as a place to eat because their meal ingredients are usually locally raised.

We started our meal with an array of antipasti including the usual sliced salamis; then focaccia, first topped with lard and then with slivers of roasted peppers; and finally a delicious salad containing raw veal and Gorgonzola. After that, the waitress wanted to know what we wanted for the primo or pasta course. They offered a trio of choices, and when we had difficulty deciding, she suggested a sample of each selection. We agreed it was a marvelous idea, and a generous parade of pasta dishes started. First we were brought ravioli with a butter sage sauce, followed by tagliolini covered with a tomato and sausage sauce, and lastly gnocchi served with a sauce made from porcini. Although we were full, the waitress convinced us that we still had enough appetite left for a little taste of that day's dessert. She then proceeded to bring us a plate containing a small sample of three, not one, delightful desserts. With the great meal we ate and the delicious wine we drank, I was expecting a rather large check, but I was pleasantly surprised by the modest one I was given. Before leaving, we purchased six bottles of wine we thought would make a nice gift for the Forneros after we left.

We got into Angelo's car and headed back to Montiglio. As we tried to drive to the pinnacle of the hill town, our way was blocked by a construction sign. We proceeded to walk up the steep hill and encountered six Chinese men repairing the road by laying down a new bed of cobblestones. They were very quick and efficient in their work. Angelo asked if we could proceed farther, and they said it would be no problem. Then Angelo surprised the Italian-speaking Chinese by speaking a few words to them in their native language. He had spent three years working in China for Fiat.

At the top of the hill were a house, a castle, and a church. The church was closed; the castle was open, but it was being prepared for a wedding, so our browsing was limited. We did get to meet the resident of the house as she helped her granddaughter carry home her schoolbooks. The woman was very friendly and told us where we could get the key to open an ancient church in the lower part of the village. The small church, San Lorenzo, is on a hill next to the cemetery; and when we got there, it was already open. Inside was a guide explaining the history of the twelfth-century church to a couple of tourists who had arrived before us; Italians treasure their antiquities. On the way home, Angelo drove us to another old structure, an abbey nestled in the hills of a huge vineyard. It also had been completed in the twelfth century and was impressively well cared for. It would not have surprised me if I had seen some monks walking the grounds.

On the way back, the Forneros told Yvonne and me that they had invited their sons and family to join us for dinner in Vestigne on Saturday. They said they were going to cook polenta, and we said we would provide a dish that would go well with this staple of Italian cooking. We went shopping late that afternoon and bought some sausage, peppers, and onions, and that evening we cooked all the ingredients along with some tomatoes. The next day Maria Teresa arrived with a beef stew to eat with the polenta she was going to prepare. She also made a trip to the nearby grocery to get some of the traditional sliced meat for the antipasti and fresh Gorgonzola. The Piedmontese finish eating their polenta by saving some in their dish to eat with Gorgonzola. The food we prepared was a big hit, and we were surprised to hear that the family had not tasted the dish before. Angelo's son, Alessandro, who has two small children, brought the customary pastries to complete the meal. The children love coming to Vestigne because the large patio has a small playhouse filled with toys and they are allowed to roam the house with little supervision.

Sunday was the day Yvonne and I were invited by Franco to join him at Vecchio Mulino, his favorite restaurant outside of Robbio. We drove there with Angelo, Maria Teresa, and Irma on a route that took us through vast fields growing Piedmont's world-famous arborio rice. The crop was ready for harvest, and the huge panoramic view of golden kernels made an impressive sight. When we arrived at the restaurant, the rest of the guests Franco had invited were there to greet us. There was Franco's sister-in-law, her brother, and her son Allessandro with his attractive wife Monica, and Monica's brother Marco. The eleven of us gathered at a long table covered with a white tablecloth and trays of bread, packets of grissini, and bottles of wine conveniently and attractively placed. Franco often eats at the place by himself, and he told Yvonne how much he was looking forward to entertaining everyone. When our son Larry and his family paid him a visit a few years earlier, Franco also assembled a large gathering for him. Larry said the meal he ate was the best he had on his visit to Italy.

I was seated beside Marco and across from Allessandro , who both spoke very good English. It was a treat not to have to depend on Yvonne to aid me in my communication. They were quite interested in American politics and the book I had written on Piedmont. I noticed that, as the parade of dishes were served, they both put modest amounts of food on their plates. It was obvious that this was a practice that helped them maintain their slim figures. I also found it to be a necessary approach to get myself through the pleasant, but demanding, task of sampling what was brought to the table.

The first antipasti consisted of a tray with five selections of cold sliced meats: duck salami, prosciutto, cooked ham, cacciatorini, and salami della duja. The cold meats were followed by insalata russa (fresh mayonnaise mixed with potatoes, peas, and carrots), quiche, a piece of cooked carrot stuffed with sweet potato, zucchini filled with mashed potato, and finally vitello tonnato.

You are able to eat all this food because the portions are small, but if you especially like something the servers are always ready to give you a second helping. After the antipasti came the primo course, panissa, which consists of risotto and beans, a dish Franco's wife made many times for Yvonne and me. The secondo course was a thin slice of roast pork served with string beans, carrots, and roast potatoes. I had eaten a little of everything that was brought to the table, but when they offered dessert, I had to give up. My diet-conscious table companions asked for macedonia, a fruit salad with liqueur. Of course, to aid in the digestive process, several of us had a *digestivo*. Angelo, who was sitting nearby, turned to me and said, "We managed to survive our strenuous chore of eating Sunday dinner at the Vecchio Mulino." As if he hadn't already done enough for us, Franco insisted as we left on buying a box of cookies made with rice dough for Yvonne to bring back to the States.

Before heading home, we made a visit to the cemetery and said some prayers for Ines; every day Franco makes this practice part of his routine. I was glad Angelo was driving because I could nod off on the way back.

That evening Clelia, a sweet and generous woman who had bought Yvonne's mother's house for her son, invited us to dinner for the next night when her daughter Giordana was going to stop by for a visit. Then she said she would come by in a short while to take us to a festival being held in a temporary building next to the grammar school just outside the village. It was a weekend for the people of Vestigue to celebrate, and on Sunday night they were having a barbecue dinner prepared for them, followed by a dance. We were interested only in observing the activities and listening to the music.

I got the feeling I was attending a wedding, because on the dance floor were people of all ages, from youngsters to senior citizens. On the stage was a five-piece band with a female vocalist, and during the whole evening, they never once stopped playing. Most of the dances were done to the Italian two-step, but there were some Latin numbers interspersed. The big surprise to me occurred when, with about thirty people on the floor, everyone spontaneously formed in a line-dance grouping and continued the somewhat intricate steps for over fifteen minutes. It all ended with a loud rendition of the popular song "YMCA."

Clelia managed to coax me into trying to dance with her. I made two circuits around the floor before I was rescued by a change in the tempo of the music. I was impressed by how well everyone danced and how much they enjoyed it. It was a long day, and Yvonne and I slept well that night.

On Monday we roamed around Ivrea, visited Renzo and Maria Teresa, and stopped in at Post Etc. to get on the Internet. We read our e-mail, and I was pleasantly surprised to find out that the Syracuse football team had beaten Northwestern.

That evening at 7:30 we walked to Clelia and Ettore's house at the end of the village. On the way we were serenaded by the barking of all the dogs protecting their fenced-in courtyards along the road. The old dog at Clelia and Ettore's house never barked, but just walked up and greeted us. When we arrived, we were taken to the modern third-floor apartment where their son, Alberto, lives. His wife and their two children were joining us for dinner, and his sister Giordana and her husband were expected later. While we were waiting, Alberto's two children, who had been music students for several years, entertained us with a duet. His daughter, Valentina, played the violin, and his son Alberto played the cello. During the evening I tried talking with Valentina, who spoke some English, and I learned she wants to be a doctor. They were quite good, and I enjoyed seeing the proud, pleased smiles on the faces of their parents.

Giordana called and said they were being delayed, and since Alberto had a commitment, we proceeded with dinner. We had the usual sliced meats followed by insalata alla russe and tonnato sauce on fresh tomatoes. The main course was polenta made from whole grain corn, which gives the dish a dark appearance and a strong flavor that was enhanced by the sauce featuring tasty sausages. The polenta was accompanied by sautéed Swiss chard, and of course, Gorgonzola and fontina were brought to the table and more polenta was heaped on the plate.

Shortly after Alberto left, his sister and her husband, Mario, arrived; since the food was still on the table, they were immediately able to dig in and satisfy their hunger. They are an interesting couple; both speak English and had worked for software companies in Milan. When Mario, who is several years older than his very pretty wife, was able to retire early, Giordana decided she would like to join him. They really didn't wish to stop working, but they wanted to live year-round in their beautiful villa at Angera on Lago Maggiore. Mario, who was an accomplished photographer, found the perfect solution when he opened a photo shop in Angera and Giordana became his helper and salesperson. They seemed so happy with their current lifestyle.

On Tuesday we decided to return to Lago Orta, where we had been in past years on two separate occasions. On the way we passed through and stopped at Borgomanero, a town with several nice shops. We felt it would be a good place to find a gift to thank the Forneros for their wonderful hospitality. At a fine china and dinnerware store, Yvonne found a very different, beautiful, modern, crystal candlestick holder. She was so pleased with her find.

The village of San Giulia, which lies opposite the island of San Giulia, is the destination of most tourists to Lago Orta. At the center of the village is a marina, with several small boats docked to take people on tours of the lake and to the densely occupied island in the middle of the small lake. Behind the marina is a petite square, bordered by several cafes and restaurants with outdoor patios to offer a grand view of the water, island, and surrounding hills. The streets leading to the piazza are narrow and filled with little shops selling touristy items. Just off the square is the Olina restaurant, a place where we had eaten five years ago, and it was our objective for a noontime meal.

On the menu was an appetizer we had eaten five years earlier, smoked tuna on a bed of dressed greens, so we ordered it again. I had remembered it was quite good. Yvonne's eating curiosity was stirred when she noticed a menu item described as a black gnocchi dish. I seldom order what she does because I often have to help clean her plate, so I had tagliatelli with a red seafood sauce. Yvonne thought her selection was interesting, but a little disappointing. That day we felt two courses were enough; we were getting concerned about the weight we might be putting on. We had a siesta of sorts by sitting in the square, where we could see all that was going on. After wandering through the narrow streets again, we made the long uphill trek to our car in the hilltop parking lot.

That evening we visited Yvonne's cousin Ida, and her son and his wife dropped in. It was an interesting evening for Yvonne as she attempted to carry on three different conversations with people who have a lot to say, while at the same time trying to keep me informed about what was going on. I noticed Yvonne's personality becomes so much more expressive and outgoing as she has to bear the main burden of interacting with people. I sometimes wonder what they think about me as I sit there just listening and having Yvonne talking for me.

During our visit we had not yet dined at our favorite restaurant in Ivrea, so on the day before we left for the airport we planned to eat at L'Aquila Antica. Near the place is a bakery that makes the best grissini Yvonne and I have ever tasted, so we decided to buy two large bags of this special treat to bring to the States. We had tasted these grissini for the first time at L'Aquila Antica on an earlier trip. In a small outdoor courtyard at the restaurant, we ate a delicious meal with porcini mushrooms featured in each course. The appetizer was a flan (mushrooms, eggs, and cream), followed by risotto with porcini, and finally the roasted fungi was served so that its soft, succulent flavor was at its best. Of course, an abundance of grissini was also consumed. While we were eating, a car drove between the patio and the backdoor entrance to the restaurant. It seems at the end of the narrow pathway was someone's garage. In Italy, space in towns can often be a problem.

On our last day at their house, the Forneros came to see us off and brought with them a dinner to share with us. We continued to be amazed at what marvelous hosts they had been. Maria Teresa loved the candlestick we presented to them, and Angelo said he would remember us every time they drank the wine we gave them. Some of our other recent neighbors also came to wish us bon voyage.

Getting to our hotel at the airport was made easy by having the hotel van pick us up. After witnessing the complicated route they took getting to the hotel, I don't think I would ever have found it. Our return to Syracuse was made easy by stopping at our son's house for a few days. The bag of grissini we gave them was really appreciated, and the breadsticks disappeared in two days. However, Larry was disappointed that we had not brought him any Gorgonzola.

When I reflected on our trip after we returned and I tried to discuss it with our friends, I realized it was not the type of venture most people would appreciate. We were not having new experiences, but renewing our connections with a culture and place that we had spent years getting to know and had become comfortable living in. Yvonne was raised in New York City but in the Piedmont culture, I came to it later in life and have learned to understand and enjoy many of its customs. In fact, I am more familiar with and remember more things about Italy, and Piedmont in particular, than I do about places from my youth. I don't know if I will ever return, but I will never forget all the memories my visits have created.

A French Barge Cruise

We had a unique and memorable vacation enjoying the cuisine, wine, and countryside ambiance while traveling on a barge.

Most people come to France to enjoy the pleasures and excitement of Paris, but there is another way to sample what the country has to offer: take a relaxing and intimate cruise on a French barge. Throughout the country are numerous canals and rivers that pass by quaint towns, historic sites, and beautiful landscapes. A barge offers lodging, wonderful hospitality, and fantastic cuisine. Your only responsibility is to relax and enjoy it all.

In 2001 three years after a trip to Spain and Morocco I took such a journey with my wife and another couple on a barge called the *Chanterelle*. I forgot how we selected this vessel, but we found it was a fortunate choice. We were picked up in Paris and bussed to the ancient city of Plagny, near the old city of Nevers where the *Chanterelle* was moored.

When I first saw the barge, I was not too impressed. It looked rather small and had a weathered and somewhat unattractive appearance. When I boarded the vessel, I passed through a cozy and elegant dining room and lounge, which hinted at what might be in store for us. Below the upper deck, the barge had ten double cabins and four singles, each with a private bathroom. If you wonder how they can squeeze this much lodging into such a little boat, the answer is simple: make the cabins a truly miniature version of a hotel room. It took a little getting used to the cramped accommodations, but it never became an annoyance.

Our good fortune arose from the fact that there were only eight passengers booked for what turned out to be a warm, sunny last week in June. With a crew of seven, it was obvious we would be well cared for. The barge's route was planned to travel north for six days, ending at a place called Rogn, only about fifty miles from where we cast off. It was a pace that allowed you to relax and enjoy your daily excursions and to fully appreciate each delicious meal that was prepared for you. Everything was extremely well organized. Sometimes you cruised between venues, while at other times you were put on board a small bus and taken to your destination while the barge continued its slow journey. The crew made sure you never missed a meal.

One day we went across a stone viaduct to a medieval village famed for its floral gardens and an impressive chateau. Another day we went on a walking tour of Nevers, a town whose history dates back to Roman times. It contains structures still standing from the Middle Ages. As a change of pace, we visited a goat cheese factory and later were given a chance to wash down the cheese at a winery producing Sancerre. Another time we went browsing through a village on market day, which is a great way to rub shoulders with the local populace and to work up an appetite for lunch. A trip to see a beautiful chateau built during the 1400s was particularly memorable, especially since we were treated to some fine-tasting wines.

Sampling French wines was one of the highlights of the trip. At each meal, two different wines were served along with a platter containing two types of cheeses. Since no selection was ever repeated, we got to sample twenty-two distinct kinds of wine and cheese. You would have to eat out a number of times in Paris to get such a diverse experience.

The wines and cheese accompanied meals that demonstrated the chef's talents and imagination. He tried to make the lunches of lighter fare, including a lot of vegetable salads and fish dishes. When he cooked, he added interest by enclosing the salmon in a sea-salt crust, and his baked ham was wrapped in a pastry crust. Since the weather was outstanding and the group was small, our lunches were served on the boat's open deck, where we could enjoy the scenery as we cruised.

The dinners were comprised of four courses, whose entrees included fish with pesto sauce, pork with prunes and polenta, lamb with a honey and sesame sauce, rabbit in a mustard sauce, and a confit of duck with mushrooms and potatoes. I guess plain old chicken is not a staple of the French diet. What were really interesting were the desserts that followed the cheese course. Included were strawberry and mango soup and mixed fruits in a champagne cream sauce. The dinner was served in an elegantly furnished dining room with a stylishly arranged table. Each night our hostess showed her talent for decorating by folding our napkins into a different and elaborate design. I was so impressed that I was reluctant to unfold my napkin. During a brief free period, the women were treated to a demonstration of this art form.

After dinner we had, at times, a chance to walk off our feasts in the town where we were moored. One night the young chef entertained us by revealing his personal decision to stop studying to be a CPA and entering a French cooking school. His enthusiasm and obvious dedication to his new career indicated he might someday achieve his ambition of being a noted French chef. It was interesting to see the very modest and small kitchen where he created all the wonderful meals he prepared. Even breakfast wasn't neglected, because each morning someone in the crew went out to purchase fresh croissants, brioche, and other pastries from the local bakery. Of course, if you were concerned about your waistline, there was also some cereal for you.

One evening, a singer and accordionist were brought on board to entertain us with some French melodies. However, the most memorable evening event for me was the balloon ride I went on with three other passengers. It took place on a bright late evening with a slight breeze blowing. The balloon was set up near our barge, and the roar of the hot-air generators drowned out the noise of the crowd that had assembled to see us off. I admit that I was a little nervous about going up in that small basket hanging below that huge balloon, but it was too late to back out.

The takeoff was exciting as the crowd cheered and we rose above our barge, which soon appeared to be rather small. Looking skyward, you were treated to panoramic views of the French countryside, where some fields were ready to be harvested and others had just been tilled. It was really breathtaking when the heater was turned off and we just floated with the breeze. I then suddenly became nervous again when I realized that we were slowly descending into a field with trees on both sides. When we could almost reach down and touch the stalks of wheat below us, the hot air was turned on and we rose sharply. The captain continued to give us a thrilling ride while he communicated with his associate, who was driving a bus around trying to follow our path and looking for a place to land. The farmers don't like it if you land on their crops.

Too soon our flight was over and we were set down in a grassy field with the bus that would return us to the barge parked nearby. Before leaving we were treated to the French ballooning tradition of drinking a glass of champagne upon completing the flight. I am sure you can understand why this event was one I will not forget.

Saying good-bye to our fellow passengers and the friendly crew who had now become our friends was difficult. The trip had been such a personal and splendid experience, and I was glad we had a few more days in Paris to help us transition from the catered world we had been in to the real one.

TWO TRADITIONAL PIEDMONT DISHES

Writing about the history and cooking of bagna cauda and risotto was of interest because eating the dishes became somewhat of a family custom.

Celebrating with a Hot Bath

The basic ingredients of bagna cauda are butter, olive oil, and anchovies and garlic that have been chopped to a fine paste. Centuries ago it was a peasant dish, and its original use was as a morning snack for the cold vineyard workers pruning vines in midwinter. They made a small fire from the vine cuttings and heated the bagna or sauce, and then dipped into the bath whatever vegetables were available in late fall and through the winter.

Have you ever wanted to add a special warmth and friendliness to a cold winter evening with your friends? Well, here is a suggestion that is both unique and simple. Ask your guests to indulge in a tradition of Piedmont, Italy, called the cult of bagna cauda. It is an eating celebration that is simple, healthy, and conducive to jovial chatter.

It is interesting to note how this dish became ubiquitous to Piedmont, a region that is landlocked and contains few olive trees. Liguria, a region on the sea to the south and with the climate for olive trees, was the source of the bagna's important ingredients. What the people of Piedmont had to offer traders who came over the Apennine Mountains with olive oil and anchovies were their delicious and plentiful wines. Brisk trade made these items cheap enough for the poor people to make the meal a staple of their diet.

Bagna cauda is not as frequently eaten as in the past, but during late autumn and winter it is enthusiastically consumed by Piedmontese who want to celebrate being Piedmontese. My mother-in-law introduced our family to the dish; and during every Christmas holiday we spent with her, she prepared the recipe that uniquely defined her roots. She would start drawing the bath before dinner when she cooked the garlic in butter and olive oil, and as the sauce slowly boiled the house would become filled with an aroma that stimulates the appetite of most Italians. The hot brew was then brought to the table in a chafing dish and set above a flame to maintain the proper temperature. On the table was a dish containing pieces of fresh vegetables like peppers, fennel, savoy cabbage, and celery. Another dish contained slices of fresh crispy Italian bread. Everyone stood around the table and took a piece of vegetable and started to take turns dipping into the bath, trying to scoop out the anchovy and garlic mixture. At times you had to battle others for the tasty scraps. The bread, which you would eat from your other hand, would catch the drippings and added to the tastiness of each bite of the food.

As we ate, there were all kinds of good-natured comments if you became too aggressive in trying to get your share. The dish was the antipasto for the rest of our meal, but my mother-in-law always tried to satisfy her appetite by eating her much-loved bagna cauda. She told my son-in-law from the south that he wouldn't be considered part of the family if he didn't learn to enthusiastically join the eating ritual. I didn't realize until many years later how ardently my daughter's family embraced the celebration. One year she was helping her daughter prepare the dish for a school project when my grandson came down the stairs; when he caught a whiff of the aroma he announced, "It smells like Christmas."

The recipe of ingredients varies quite a bit and seems to depend on how much one likes anchovies and garlic. I have seen where a head of garlic, a tablespoon of butter, one-half cup of olive oil, and two anchovy filets are suggested for one person; to where only two cloves of garlic, five tablespoons of butter, six tablespoons of olive oil, and three and a half ounces of anchovies are specified for four persons. I would recommend a head of garlic and a can of anchovy filets for four people as a compromise, but as you can see, one has a lot of discretion in preparing the dish.

If you wish to add some elegance to your celebration, you can provide each person with a small pottery bowl for dipping. Of course, all the conflict and competition would be eliminated, and the party might not be as good-humored. However you host your friends, you will find that this idea of an Italian fondue party will be entertaining and give a warm, comfortable feeling to your guests.

Cooking Risotto

Risotto is a rice dish that took centuries to evolve. The Chinese may have first cultivated rice, but the Italians have made growing it and cooking it an art form. It all starts with producing rice that absorbs liquid without becoming soggy, and results in a creamy morsel of food that is firm to the bite.

One of the few places in the world where this rice, called arborio, is grown is in the Po Valley of Piedmont, Italy. The area has ideal topography for growing rice. It is surrounded on three sides by mountains, whose winter runoff drains into a flat plain that retains the water. Many years ago what was a wasteland started to be reclaimed by religious orders; and over the centuries, through canal digging, irrigation, and applying fertilizer, the land was turned into a rich landscape for rice cultivation. Today, Italy is Europe's largest rice producer; half of it is grown in Piedmont, and what was originally a labor-intensive farming process is now highly mechanized.

The technique employed in cooking risotto is to force-feed the grains of rice by adding small amounts of broth and then stirring the mixture until it reaches its creamy state. The rice dishes of other cultures are cooked by adding the liquid at the beginning and letting it be absorbed by the grain. How the technique was developed is not known, but once you have tasted rice cooked this way you are disappointed by other methods.

The basic ingredients of risotto are onions softened in olive oil or butter, arborio rice, wine, and broth; when the mixture is cooked, you add Parmesan cheese. It sounds simple, but it requires patience and attention. And the variety of possible recipes that can be cooked is limited only by one's culinary imagination.

Now let's get practical and give some specific hints on cooking risotto. Most recipes have some ingredients added to those mentioned earlier. In selecting what to add, you should first decide how you will be serving it—as an appetizer, as a starch, or as the main course. In Italy, it is almost always served as the first course, while in American restaurants it is often an accompaniment to a meat or fish dish. In our house it was usually the main course and served with a salad.

The vegetables that can be added include peas, chopped-up spinach, broccoli, fennel, mushrooms, squash, zucchini, tomatoes, cauliflower, savoy cabbage, and peppers. The meats can include pieces of prosciutto, pancetta, sausage, chicken, chicken livers, beef, and leftover cooked meat, while shrimp also makes a nice addition. The liquid employed is usually chicken broth, but beef, fish, or vegetable broths or even plain water can also be used. I have also used the liquid derived from soaking dried mushrooms or canned tomatoes. Besides Parmesan, you can add Gorgonzola, mozzarella, or fontina cheeses.

I am going to describe an all-purpose recipe that will guide you in completing the dish regardless of what ingredients you may want to use. Don't worry, because precision in measuring quantities is not critical.

Depending on how you will serve the dish, two cups of uncooked rice will serve from four to six people with good appetites. Select a pot large enough to hold the rice expanded by about eight cups of liquid and other ingredients you may want to add. Heat up two tablespoons of butter or olive oil and soften one medium onion that has been finely chopped. Before adding the rice, you will want to sauté any uncooked meat you are going to use, and in some cases, vegetables like mushrooms or zucchini can also be sautéed at this time. After the rice is added, stir the mixture for a couple of minutes to toast the grains, to coat them with the oil that prevents the kernels from absorbing the liquid too quickly.

Now it is time to add the wine, about one-half cup for two cups of rice. (Don't worry: some recipes even suggest more.) Cook for two minutes to evaporate the alcohol. Sometimes I stop cooking at this point to hold the mixture so I can better control when I finish. Risotto should be eaten right after it is cooked.

At this point you can start to add the hot broth. I found the microwave is convenient for heating whatever liquid you will be adding. Some cooks leave a pot simmering on the stove. Add a small amount of broth and stir to ensure that all the grains can share the liquid. Keep putting in small amounts of liquid and stirring after each addition.

During the simmering process you may want to add some other ingredients—for instance, fresh chopped-up spinach, cabbage, or frozen peas. Some vegetables—like broccoli, cauliflower, or fennel—will need to be cooked a bit before adding them to the rice.

When the mixture reaches its creamy state, or the consistency you want, it is now ready for the finishing process, which traditionally includes adding a generous helping of Parmesan cheese. For additional flavor or to make the dish creamier, you can put in a couple of tablespoons of butter, Gorgonzola, or mozzarella.

The traditions associated with risotto also include the manner of eating it. When you scoop out a portion of risotto from a serving dish, it is piping hot. The first thing Italians do is use their fork to compress the mound, so that more Parmesan cheese can be sprinkled on the rice. Then they start eating from the outside of the compressed surface, which is not as hot. My daughter once had dinner at a restaurant with an associate she had just met and they both ordered risotto. When the dish was served, she noticed he immediately flattened it and went through the process she knew so well. A cultural bond was formed, and they proceeded to reminisce about their family life.

The joy of cooking risotto is the freedom to be creative without depending on recipes and seeing it grow into the succulent and delicious dish it becomes while you tend to its cooking. For me, added delight came from realizing I was preparing my wife and mother-in-law's favorite dish and observing their pleasure and hearing their compliments.

Ines: A Life that Spans an Ocean

My long association with Ines led to me bonding with her homeland and developing an appreciation of my Italian heritage.

Preface

Ines was my mother-in-law, whom I got to know better than my own mother. After all, if someone lives to be ninety-eight years old and spends part of her last thirty years living with you, getting to know the person becomes quite simple. At dinnertime she would tell me about various aspects of her life; what she might have intended to overlook or wanted to forget, my wife, Yvonne, would fill in for me. Her outspoken ways did not inspire affection, but her determination and hardworking attitude commanded respect. I always loved how she responded to some criticism or rebuke my wife or I would make: "That's the way God made me." Not wanting to challenge a work of God seemed to end any further discussion.

What I write about her early years reflects what she told me and Yvonne. My wife knew her mother quite well and added some interpretation to events that gave me most of my insights to Ines's early life. Later I was able to form my own opinion, but Yvonne often had a view that added to my understanding.

My wife and I both loved Ines, and although her traits and view of life often added stress to our lives, she also added a spirit that showed what hard work and a focused attitude could accomplish. Writing about her was something that I often thought about doing, and I hope that my recollections show that she was what is often referred to as an unforgettable character. Her attachment to her homeland helped foster in me an awareness of my Italian heritage, which eventually led to a greater appreciation of Italy and things Italian. My wife valued her skill in cooking, sewing, and knitting, which contributed to reducing my wife's household burden when she went back to school and work. Ines tried hard to make herself a contributing member of our family. Both of us have many memories that we share about Ines that made her an important element in our lives

From Lyon to New York City

Ines's mother, Maria, and her sister, Angela, grew up in Masino, a small village perched on the ridge of a moraine in Piedmont, Italy. Its one claim to fame is that it includes a centuries-old castle that housed the families of past rulers of the area. The village looks down a steep slope filled with grape arbors to the slightly larger village of Vestigne, which has a tall bell tower and a large church to distinguish itself. This is where Ines's father, Luigi, one of eleven children, was born and raised. In the late nineteenth century, most people in these villages supported themselves by farming as a tenant or as the proud owner of a small piece of land. However, many others found that at times additional means were required to fulfill their basic needs. Ines's family decided that crossing the Alps into France could provide opportunities not found in Italy.

Ines tells a story about her father, who as a young man set out for France by foot to find some work. When traveling through the Alps, he encountered a storm and became lost. As he was struggling and ready to give up hope, he was found by the legendary St. Bernard dogs, whose masters gave him refuge at their monastery. After a couple of days to recover from his life-threatening experience, he continued his journey to Lyon, France, where he found employment as a construction worker. He returned years later with some savings and met Maria when she came down to Vestigne for a village dance. After a short courtship they were married, and soon after along came Umberto, followed shortly by a second son, Ubaldo. With extra mouths to feed, Luigi decided that he had to take his family back to Lyon to earn a livelihood. It was there that Ines came into this world in 1904.

She was always so proud of being born in France because, years later when she immigrated to the United States, it set her apart from the other Italian emigrants. She came in under a different quota and didn't have to be processed through Ellis Island. When Ines was eighteen months old, her father decided to return to Italy and raise his family in Turin. At that time the city was beginning to lead Italy into a more prosperous period, and Luigi wanted to return to his roots. In addition, Maria's unmarried sister, Angela, was living there with her parents, so there was family to give them support in the unfamiliar urban environment of Turin. Ines's unmarried aunt provided her with so much kindness and attention in her early years that she remembered her with a great deal of fondness throughout her life. It was a sad day for Ines when her father again decided to return to Vestigne.

Ines never talked much about the years that followed; during all the times we returned to Vestigne, she never showed my wife and me where she lived. We can only surmise from what we learned later about the village that living was quite primitive. Ines was not proud of her early existence, but I never heard her complain about these years. She was probably trying to forget this time in her life.

She seemed to remember with clarity when she reached the age of sixteen and was able to get a job in a fabric mill in Ivrea, a town of about 25,000 compared to the 800 or so people residing in Vestigne. The town is located only about six miles away from Vestigne; but at that time, regular bus service didn't exist and Ines didn't own a bike, so she lived in a dormitory like other women in her situation. Ines worked hard, and at the age of eighteen was given responsibility for running her own loom. A picture of her in front of the large machine she ran shows a smile; the expression on her face reflects the pride she felt. On the weekends she walked home to Vestigne to join her mother, who was now living by herself since her father and two brothers were again off working in France.

During World War I, Luigi had the unenviable and dangerous military assignment of being a medic on the battlefield. Witnessing the suffering and death that surrounded him did things to his psyche and he was given drugs to relieve the stress. For the rest of his life he was a different person, and his physical strength had diminished. With him and his two sons working, they were able to support themselves and send some money home to help Maria and Ines.

Living and working in Ivrea gave Ines the opportunity to develop other interests. She went each week to attend a town dance and met several young men who appreciated her talent for the pastime. One man in particular became a partner who advanced her interest in her favorite leisure activity. Together they went through routines that provoked the attention of other dancers who often stopped to admire them. She often told Yvonne how much she enjoyed her nights being the belle of the ball.

One night a new face appeared at the dance. He was Lorenzo Ganio, a handsome young man who was very graceful on the ballroom floor. Noting Ines's talent, he wanted to test his skill with her, and soon they were spending the whole evening together. He became a regular at the dance and spent all of his time with Ines. Years later I was able to personally witness the dancing prowess that Yvonne told me about her parents when I saw them dance at our wedding. The smoothness and gracefulness of their movements really surprised me.

To a village girl like Ines, Lorenzo was an impressive person. He was born in Ivrea, and after apprenticing to be a cobbler, he decided at the age of fifteen to seek his fortune by joining his brother and sisters in New York City. He started working in a restaurant as a kitchen gofer, and after awhile he advanced to being a vegetable sous-chef. However, he then realized that being a waiter offered the opportunity for more money for less hours of working. After many years making a living in New York, he discovered that he had a problem. Unless he returned to Italy to serve his time in the Italian army, he risked possible arrest if he ever wanted to return. So in 1922 Lorenzo went back to Italy to fulfill his six-month duty of being a soldier and was stationed near his hometown where he found it easy to attend town dances.

He was a gregarious young man who, like many Italian men, liked to exaggerate his position in life. He painted a rosy picture of his family's success in New York and the opportunities that were available. Italians have always thought of America as being the land of riches. I know Ines, a young lady of eighteen from the poor small village of Vestigne, would have been impressed, not only by his dancing, but also by his lineage. Before he left Italy, Lorenzo proposed to Ines and promised that when he had saved enough money, he would send for her. It was obvious that Lorenzo didn't possess great wealth, because it took two years to have Ines join him. At the age of twenty, she left Italy to settle in the land of plenty known as Stati Uniti.

A Long Road to Motherhood

When Ines arrived in America, she moved into an apartment with Lorenzo's married sister, Maria, and his then-unmarried sister, Elisa. Lorenzo had lived with these family members since he arrived eight years earlier, and he was now awaiting his future bride at his own nearby apartment. Two days later they began life as husband and wife. Ines had left a primitive existence in Vestigne, but she wasn't exactly entering the lap of luxury in her new home. The lower west side at that time was a place of walk-up tenements of small apartments with running water, but no private toilet facilities. Life was not easy, and wives without children would go out to work. Ines got along extremely well with her sisters-in-law, and Maria helped her get a job in a garment factory. At that time it was a place where lots of women could find work. As she had in the past, Ines adapted well and was soon an important financial contributor to the Ganio household.

After a couple years of working, Ines was ready to have a child; but Lorenzo, like many Italian men I met in Piedmont, wanted no part of fatherhood. (These men, I knew, changed in their declining years and expressed regret about their attitude toward children.) With two salaries to live on, Ines and Lorenzo decided they wanted to leave the crowded inhospitable environment of the tenements to settle into the suburbs. Astoria, Queens, was then considered to be in the suburbs, but an elevated train line running through it provided convenient ready access to what was known as the city. The apartments were not large, but they offered private toilet facilities and sometimes a small backyard. Many friends from the old country lived in Astoria, and so a tight-knit community of Piedmontese-speaking people was formed.

With two incomes, Ines and Lorenzo were able to save some money and even invested some in America's prospering economy. In the summer of 1929, they were ready for a proud return to Piedmont. Lorenzo's sister, Maria, and her husband had returned earlier and were now the owners of a small grocery store in Ivrea; while his brother, Dominick, and his wife also went back and leased a building in Ivrea where they ran a hotel and a restaurant. So the family had been successful in New York City and had made a triumphant return home. Ines and Lorenzo enjoyed their short stay visiting their family and probably anticipating their own future successful return to Italy. However, all thought of continued good fortune collapsed a short time later with the advent of the depression. Lorenzo had lost a little money, and from that time on wanted no part of investments outside of a savings bank.

Although life had improved for Ines, there was still something missing: an offspring. After ten years of being married, she finally convinced Lorenzo they should have a child. Many of their friends were also entering parenthood, so it was becoming the thing to do. On September 14, 1934, Ines gave birth to Yvonne and left the workforce to take care of her. She stayed home for four years caring for her daughter; but the family, in spite of their very frugal ways, was now spending their small savings since Lorenzo's wages just weren't enough to support them properly. His lack of earning power was a constant source of conflict in their marriage. Ines had always felt misled by Lorenzo's original optimistic portrayal of her future with him. Her frequent reminders of his shortcomings would then elicit from him angry words of self–defense, and heated arguments would take place. Criticism and harsh words plagued them throughout their marriage. However, like many in their generation, they worked around these conflicts and accepted them as part of marriage. The alternative of divorce was too difficult and embarrassing to undertake.

Reluctantly, Ines accepted her fate and recognized she would have to return to work, but she needed someone to take care of Yvonne. Her mother, Maria, at that time was still living in Vestigne, but there were considerable changes in her life that would make her receptive to Ines's request for help. Maria's husband had died at the early age of forty-two from what was thought to be the effects of his service during World War I. Her son Umberto was married and living nearby, but Baldo was again working in France, so she was living alone. She managed to make some money doing laundry and her children were also helping support her, but being a healthy woman of sixty-one she was probably looking for more from life. So when Ines asked her to come to America and help raise Yvonne, she looked at it as an opportunity to bring some renewed interest into her life.

Ines went back to work, and Maria slept on the couch in a three-room apartment; Yvonne, who slept in her parents' room, began life under the watchful eye of her grandmother. At the time, Yvonne spoke only the Piedmont dialect, which was fortunate because Maria obviously spoke the same language, along with the French she had learned while living in that country. Yvonne developed a wonderful relationship with her grandmother, who was quite different from her mother. Ines was a serious woman who didn't seem to know how to have fun and was reserved with her affection. Maria was more relaxed and not sensitive to what other people thought about her, so she was more comfortable in expressing herself. Although Maria and her daughter both practiced their Catholic faith, Maria had a more personal relationship with her God. When walking with Yvonne and passing a church, she would always make a point of stopping to make a short visit. Religion for her was not a set of practices, but a true spiritual feeling.

When Yvonne was not in school, she went everywhere with her grandmother, who in spite of not speaking any English, found friends who spoke her dialect or French. Maria helped her daughter's marriage survive and gave to her granddaughter the guidance of someone with a drastically different view of life.

Coping with a Maturing Daughter

Although Ines had been in America for ten years when her daughter was born, she felt her command of English made her a poor mentor for teaching the language to Yvonne. To relieve her and her husband of any stress in communicating, both parents only spoke the Piedmontese dialect to Yvonne. Since all their friends took the same basic approach with their children, there were no problems when families would visit each other. When Yvonne was almost ready to enter school, Ines realized she had to do something to prepare for the big change in her daughter's life. Someone suggested that there might be some kind of prekindergarten class Yvonne could attend. Ines made an appointment with the grammar school principal and explained the situation. The principal was quite sympathetic and enrolled Yvonne in a class six months before she was scheduled to enter school. Spending eighteen months in kindergarten was just what Yvonne needed to prepare for entering the American culture.

Yvonne was an extremely bright student. She would finish her assigned work in class and then take out a book and read. Ines was told about her brilliant daughter, but she didn't fully appreciate or understand all she was being told. Instead of praising Yvonne for reading so much, Ines often criticized her for not having other interests. However, she was proud that Yvonne was put into the rapid curriculum. After several terms in these advanced classes, Yvonne was skipped one term to further challenge her abilities.

Several years after Yvonne entered school, Ines found a nearby four-room flat on the second floor of a six-family apartment house. Now Yvonne moved into a room that she shared with her grandmother. The apartment had a small kitchen, with room for a table that could squeeze four people around it. A pantry contained a refrigerator adjacent to a tiny bathroom. The living room extended the width of the apartment, with two closets at one end and two windows at the other end. One door from the room led to Ines and Lorenzo's bedroom, and the other to a small room where Yvonne and her grandmother slept. It was a rent-controlled apartment, which meant the rent was very reasonable and the owner had great difficulty raising it.

The life of Ines's family each week followed a very simple routine. Ines left early each weekday to work as a seamstress. Lorenzo left later to serve as a waiter at a Wall Street restaurant. Each day he would return for a short time to be with Yvonne when she came home from school. He would then return to the restaurant for the evening meal and arrive back home after nine o'clock. Maria would spend some of her time each day preparing the noonday meal she shared with Yvonne. Supper was a lighter meal, which the three ladies usually shared together. The weekend was the time for family togetherness, especially on Sunday, the occasion for a family feast. Lorenzo would usually share a sweet Manhattan with one of his friends in the neighborhood while Ines was working in the kitchen. Since the kitchen was too small to comfortably accommodate everyone, Lorenzo would set up a folding table in the living room with a white tablecloth with place settings and bread and grissini distributed among them. In the center was a large lazy Susan to hold all the antipasti dishes Ines would bring out of her refrigerator. She always prepared more food than would be consumed that day. The first course would be followed by some type of pasta dish, and then came the meat course with a vegetable. The idea was to have enough leftovers to provide food for the following week. Many Sundays the meal was shared with one of their Piedmont friends.

Frugality and saving money was a lifetime passion for Ines. Lorenzo's wages went to pay the rent and put food on the table. The money Ines earned was mostly put in the bank and paid for little incidentals and some frivolities, like going to the movies. Clothing was not a big expense since Ines made most of the clothes for herself and Yvonne; but when she had to go into a store to buy something, she made sure that she got her money's worth.

When Yvonne was growing up, it was very popular to wear a pea jacket. To please her daughter, Ines took her shopping to buy one. Yvonne found just what she wanted, but they were a little expensive and Ines thought she would soon grow out of the jacket. She made Yvonne try on a bigger size, which she bought her since she could wear it for several years. When Yvonne wore it to school, her American friends, of course, teased her about the nice pea *coat* she was wearing. In spite of being in this country for many years,

Ines's childhood gave her little ability to understand the wardrobe needs of a growing American child. For her, having clean warm clothes on your back was all that was necessary.

On another occasion, a friend gave Yvonne several blouses as gifts. Ines thought they were such good buys that she purchased some more for Yvonne, and her daughter wound up with five of them. All the blouses were cut the same, but were made different by the designs that were painted on them. The blouses were nice, but not the style for a young teenager. Since they were a loose-fitting design, Yvonne got several years of use out of them and Ines didn't have to buy any new ones. To Ines, her daughter possessed a rather large set of varied attire for school; she couldn't understand why Yvonne after awhile was reluctant to wear one of her many blouses.

Ines did at times spend money to make her daughter happy, and on one occasion she succeeded. Yvonne always remembered with fondness the three years she spent at a summer camp with her friend, Lucy. However, sometimes the results of her generosity did not turn out as joyful. After hearing many requests from Yvonne for a bicycle, Ines finally agreed to buy her one. However, because of a fear of having Yvonne ride it in Astoria, she had it delivered to a friend's farm in New Jersey. A couple of times a year, the family went to the farm and Yvonne was allowed to ride the bike by herself on a short dirt road. Ines always wondered why Yvonne didn't show an appreciation for having her own bicycle.

Ines continued to save her money and had enough to buy a house, like many of her friends were doing. She was willing to take the plunge, but Lorenzo wanted no part of such an undertaking. His reluctance to buy a house was probably motivated somewhat by the idea that he wanted to return to Italy. The war in Europe had ended, Italy was recovering from that disaster, and contacts were again being established with one's family. By 1950 both Lorenzo and Maria were experiencing the lure of returning to their roots. Maria had managed to learn enough English to become an American citizen, but she missed her homeland. She was in her early seventies and felt if she passed away in the United States, God wouldn't be able to find her. Ines reluctantly agreed with her mother and provided the money to buy her a small house in Vestigne. It was a way of paying Maria back for all she had done in caring for her daughter. When her son Baldo, who worked in France during the war, heard about her plans to return to Italy, he decided that he should help ease her waning years by living with her. Although Maria leaving would relieve the congestion in the apartment, everyone was sorry to see her go. Yvonne, who had spent so much time with her grandmother, was especially sad.

Soon after Maria left in the spring of 1950, Lorenzo felt it was time for him to also return. After his daughter, who was fifteen years old, finished the school year, Lorenzo and Yvonne packed their bags and set sail for Italy. At that time the way to Italy was through Paris, by train to Turin and then Ivrea. After their arrival in Lorenzo's hometown, they stayed at the one-star hotel run by his brother and his wife. It was time for him to renew his relationship with his cronies from the past, and that is what he did for the whole summer. His neglected daughter found amusement with the engineers from Olivetti who stayed at her uncle's hotel. She discovered that an attractive American girl was of great interest to young Italian men, and she spent many evenings being amused and flattered by their attention. She also managed to convince her father that she should go on a short tour to Rome, Naples, and Capri with the wife of her mother's cousin. Yvonne was growing up fast without the watchful eye of her mother.

When Yvonne first arrived, she was shocked by the primitive conditions under which her grandmother and uncle were living. The house had a dirt floor, no running water, an outhouse, and corn husks for a mattress. However, after several visits she realized they were happy together because family and familiar surroundings were more important than some of life's luxuries. Bonding with her uncle was especially satisfying; after many lonely years in France, he was reuniting with his family. Yvonne fondly remembers Baldo teaching her and singing to her some French songs.

Yvonne returned to America with an understanding of her parents' heritage, but more importantly, recognizing her growth as a young lady. She would now be more assertive in the presence of her mother.

Ines was swollen with pride that her daughter had graduated high school at the tender age of sixteen and was preparing to enter Queens College to major in languages. Lorenzo, like many Italian men, felt higher education was not necessary for women. The daughters of Ines's friends had gone to business schools and then obtained jobs in offices as they traveled a somewhat different life path than her Yvonne. Ines felt it was now her turn to return to Italy and visit and introduce Yvonne to her family. They took the same route to Italy and also stayed at her uncle's hotel in Ivrea. However, this experience of being in Italy was quite different for Yvonne than the visit with her father. Her mother had a much bigger family, and some lived in the large city of Turin, which was not far from Ivrea. Ines took Yvonne everywhere she went, and strong connections were made with many caring Italians. But always being with Ines limited Yvonne's opportunities for independent adventures.

Ines stayed and visited with her mother and brother on several occasions, but she was not appalled by the conditions under which they lived like Yvonne was when she visited two years earlier. Ines's vivid memories of her early childhood probably jaded her attitude toward her mother's situation. Ines returned home with her attachment to Italy renewed and her daughter having developed some of the same affection for the country. Ines had visions of coming back again sometime soon.

Ines's future started to undergo a significant change when her daughter started to date me for the first time. I was an Italian, but really more of an American since my parents were born in this country. In addition, I had a blotch on my past since my grandparents came from Sicily, a place not thought of fondly by mainland Italians. But being a graduate engineering student seemed to erase this blemish on my credentials.

When I started dating Yvonne, I spent only brief moments with Ines, so I had no idea about her attitude toward me. After several months of dating, Yvonne surprised me and her parents. She wanted to study in Italy during her junior year in college. Her past visits had instilled in her a desire to further explore the culture and her place in it. Her mother was probably ecstatic about her wishes and heartily agreed with them.

It turned out that the ensuing months led to impressions and feelings that made us all aware of where our futures would lie. Yvonne was disappointed in Italian schooling, and though she met an admirer she decided that life in a place like Ivrea was too limiting and provincial. I missed Yvonne and through our letters gained insights that told me she was the woman I wanted to marry. Ines now knew her daughter was different from those of her friends, who all became romantically connected with men from Piedmont. It was my good fortune that Yvonne was going to follow a way more in keeping with an American lifestyle.

Almost immediately after Yvonne returned to the States, I proposed getting engaged and she accepted. Ines didn't know me that well, and what she did know about me didn't fit into her ideas of what made for an ideal son-in-law. I knew nothing about her culture, I didn't speak Italian, and I might take Yvonne away from New York City. She probably anticipated her family losing its connection with Piedmont. Within weeks after Yvonne returned from Italy, I was drafted into the army and wound up at Fort Bliss in El Paso, Texas. Ines probably thought that this distant separation might test our resolve.

A few months after I arrived at my residence in Texas, unpleasant events occurred for both Ines and me. Ines's mother was seriously ill, and my mother had to undergo an operation for a brain tumor. Ines immediately made plans to go see her mother, and she wanted Yvonne to accompany her. Yvonne had gone to work when she returned from studying in Italy and had tentative plans to return to college in the fall. But she also wanted to see her grandmother, so postponing her education didn't upset her. My short time in the army didn't entitle me to enough leave to come home; fortunately, my mother's operation was a success.

Ines and Yvonne's sojourn became rather complicated. They spent almost two months trying to comfort Maria, but they realized that she might linger for a much longer time, so they made plans to return home. They set sail from Genoa in December, when the bursitis Ines had been suffering from in Ivrea flared up and became much worse. The ship's doctor said the crossing in winter would be rough and her condition could get even nastier. He advised getting off the boat in Naples and returning to Ivrea. Yvonne found a hotel for her mother and took care of her while she rested and the pain subsided. After two days, Ines felt well enough to return by train to Ivrea; and after a few more weeks of rest, she was ready to again get on a boat for America.

During this time Yvonne and I spent a lot of time writing and feeling the frustration of our separation. I felt there was an option we should explore. In the army battery I was assigned to were a number of drafted college graduates who were married and had their wives with them and living off the base. It seemed like a wonderful alternative to living in the barracks and writing letters every day. Yvonne agreed that getting married while I was still in the army was a better idea than finishing college, and she approached Ines about planning the event. Ines couldn't understand why we were in such a rush; after all, she waited two years to get married after being proposed to. Ines finally relented and started to make some plans when her mother passed away. Ines and Yvonne were glad they had spent so much time with Maria before she died and realized the comfort they had been able to give made her death easier to accept.

Ines was paying the bills for the wedding, but Yvonne was making the plans and the arrangements. I returned in July three days before the scheduled date. Though things were quite hectic at times, I managed to get my wedding ring fitted and bought a car for our return to El Paso.

I saw very little of Ines before the wedding, and I think she was more nervous than happy. When the day came and all her friends were there to celebrate with her, she seemed quite pleased with all the arrangements Yvonne had made. The hotel was impressive, the meal was delicious, and her daughter looked beautiful. It was a moment for Ines to be proud as her friends offered their congratulations.

Later, when Yvonne and I were leaving on our honeymoon, I made Ines unhappy as we said farewell. I embraced her, but I couldn't call her "Mama." I had not had much contact with her and, coupled with her previous lack of expressing affection, it was awkward for me to address her as I did my own mother. When I left, she was in tears, and it took me a long time to repair the damage.

Becoming a Grandmother

While Yvonne was in El Paso she wrote often to Ines, and several weeks after her arrival sent her a picture of her happily married daughter. To Ines she didn't look too happy, because Yvonne looked much thinner than when she was under Ines's care. Summers in El Paso are very hot, and Yvonne lost some of her appetite and a little weight. I had never noticed, but Ines did. In a couple of weeks a large package arrived, filled with some antipasti Ines had made along with some salami, which she knew Yvonne loved to eat. The food was accompanied by a letter admonishing Yvonne for neglecting herself and me for not taking proper care of her daughter. We enjoyed Ines's generosity and Yvonne continued to write regularly to her mother, but she didn't include any more pictures.

Yvonne had good news for Ines when one of her letters explained that I was planning to return to school at New York University and would be discharged three months before my two-year draft period expired. In addition, she mentioned that I had been offered a teaching position for the spring semester and we would be living at my parents' house. When Yvonne got a job soon after our arrival, Ines was envisioning us settling into life in New York City. The next few months made Ines especially happy. Yvonne would drop in and eat with her while I was going to night classes, and on Sunday the families would get together for dinner. It was a lifestyle that pleased our parents, but having sampled the small-town environment of El Paso made living in the big city less appealing to Yvonne and me. Neither of our parents was pleased when we announced our decision to accept a job with the General Electric Company in Syracuse, New York. To our parents, the five-hour bus ride from New York City seemed like a long journey to see us, but over the years Ines and Lorenzo made the trip on many occasions. My mother's health after her operation limited her ability to travel, and my parents made few trips to see us, so we tried to please them by making numerous visits back to New York City.

We arrived in Syracuse in early June 1956 and moved into a furnished apartment. Ines wasted no time in coming to see us and arrived with Lorenzo for the Fourth of July weekend. By October we moved into a three-room apartment that we furnished ourselves. After we returned home for Thanksgiving, Ines and Lorenzo came back again to spend Christmas with us and see our new home. These reciprocating short visits continued until our daughter, Susan, was born in June 1957, when Ines came to spend six weeks helping Yvonne with our firstborn. Yvonne believed Ines enjoyed caring for her first grandchild so much that she was in no rush to return home. Summer was a slow work period where Ines was employed, and she had no trouble taking time off.

Soon after Susan was born we bought our first house, and in August 1959 our son Larry was born. Ines came to spend three weeks helping Yvonne. Ines thought we now had the perfect family—one daughter and one son. None of the children of her friends or relatives had larger families. When Ray, our third child, was born eighteen months later in February, Ines was a bit upset and came to spend only one week helping Yvonne. If we had had another child, I 'm not sure how long Ines would have spent with us.

When Ines came to help Yvonne with Susan, she also tried to contribute to my chores around the house. During her first visit, I decided to paint the house. I would get up on the ladder to scrape off the peeling paint, while Ines stood on the ground with her scraper preparing the siding for painting. On the weekend I gave her a brush and a pail of paint, and she spent two days spreading paint on whatever surfaces she could reach from the ground. With her help, I was able to finish the job in one weekend.

When Ines was in Syracuse helping after Ray was born, a snowstorm occurred, and she felt the need to help me clear the driveway. Fortunately I had two shovels, and we made short work of removing the snow. This was a task she always approached with pride. Even years later when I had a snowblower, she insisted on coming out to help me. She claimed when she shoveled there was no trace of snow left, whereas my blower left some around to spoil the black appearance of our driveway. I also thought she wanted to impress our neighbors with her industriousness. It was always obvious that Ines wanted to keep busy and help whenever she could.

During these years we got together with Ines and Lorenzo on many occasions, even going on vacations with each other. We frequently went to New York City and stayed at their small four-room apartment because my mother and father found it difficult to accommodate three little children and two more grown-ups at their flat.

It was a cozy and somewhat exciting experience spending a weekend at Ines's place. For sleeping accommodations, one chair opened into a bed for our Susan and a small slab couch served as a bed for Larry. For Ray, our youngest, Ines kept a small folding cot, which she brought up from the basement. Yvonne and I slept in her old bedroom on a sofa that opened into a double bed. It was a very compact arrangement; no one was more than ten feet from someone else. It was very easy to restore the array of sleeping places for daytime living. When it was time for dinner, Lorenzo would pull out a tablecloth and set up his folding aluminum table in the living room; then Ines would bring to it an appetizing selection of her dishes.

Our weekends were always filled with much socializing. We would spend some time with my parents, but most of the action would occur at my in-laws' apartment. There were many Piedmont friends living in Astoria, and over the course of a weekend many would pay us a visit. Lorenzo was always ready with his offer of vermouth, and the visitors would make a fuss over our family. The children would sleep well in the car on the ride home.

When our children were two, four, and six years old, a decisive change to my family was about to occur, and Ines gave us support that made a vital contribution to our lives. A few weeks before Christmas, I explained to Yvonne that the project I was working on at General Electric was going to require me to spend at least six months in remote eastern Turkey to assist in installing a very long-range tracking radar to observe Russian missile launches.

Yvonne's reaction expressed the burden she would have to face in raising our family: "Except for a few days when you have been out of town, we have never been apart. It will be lonely being here alone for so long."

Being alone with three children seemed like a paradox, but I understood what she was saying. Who would help her care for the children and the house? All I could think to say was, "Maybe your mother could come up and spend some time with you." We decided to broach the subject with Ines and Lorenzo when they came up to spend Christmas with us.

After a nice dinner prepared by Yvonne and Ines and several glasses of wine, I started to bring up the problem we were having. "I want to tell you that in May of next year, I will be going to Turkey for six months."

Before I could continue on with my story, Ines interrupted me and said, "What a coincidence. Papa and I are planning to spend that time returning to Italy."

Yvonne said, "Now both my husband and parents will be deserting me."

Seeing how upset her daughter was, Ines almost immediately said, "Why don't you and the children come with us?"

Yvonne could hardly believe her ears and said, "You are not kidding, are you?" Since Ines scarcely ever joked, she didn't even need an answer. Right away she said, "When do we leave?"

The rest of the day was spent discussing plans for the trip. I was going to rent a Volkswagen car to be delivered in Italy. Ines was going to book passage for a ship leaving in April and ask relatives in Ivrea to try and locate an apartment to rent.

Yvonne spent several months planning what to take to Italy for her and the children. One item that turned out to be a great idea was an inflatable swimming pool for the children. There was at that time nothing like that in Italy, and bathing in it became the favorite pastime of the children. I transported my family and their entire luggage to the boat; and as it departed I realized that I, not Yvonne, was the one who would now have to face each day alone.

Yvonne had made several crossings of the Atlantic Ocean and was very careful in attending to the children's needs and safety while on the ship. Ines really wasn't much help because she was a poor sailor despite her numerous voyages. Upon their arrival in Genoa, Cousin Angelo was waiting with a truck to transport everyone to Ivrea. They were all going to stay at Aunt Illa's hotel until an apartment could be found. The dwelling was really not suitable for small children, so when Angelo announced he might have located an apartment, everyone was ecstatic.

The rental was an unfurnished, two-bedroom apartment in a brand-new development. It was suitable if furniture could be obtained to make it livable. Again Cousin Angelo came to the rescue. He knew a place where you could buy furniture with the understanding that it would be returned when it wasn't needed anymore. It is amazing how accommodating Italian merchants can be in dealing with customers. Few items are furnished in Italian apartments, so a secondhand refrigerator and stove and lighting fixtures were purchased. Ines's sister-in-law generously supplied kitchenware from her hotel and restaurant. The apartment was very basic, but they managed. Ines and Lorenzo occupied one bedroom, while the children slept in the other bedroom; Susan and Larry were in a bed, and Ray once again found himself in a crib. Yvonne's boudoir was the living-room couch.

Yvonne was able to cope with the problems she encountered as she settled into life in Ivrea because she was fluent in both Italian and the Piedmont dialect. Whenever the children were exposed to the local environment, Yvonne was with them and translated the conversations that occurred. After a short time, Susan and Larry got enrolled in a daycare run by the nuns and they got a chance to be on their own. Since Ray was alone for a good part of the day, he became an appendage to his mother by wrapping his arms around her legs whenever they were alone.

At school the children fit in because the nuns were so caring and attentive. In fact, on all occasions when the children met grown-ups they felt very comfortable. Italians were always very expressive in the warmth they showed toward them, and the children readily sensed it and felt welcome. An interesting situation arose at school one day that showed Susan and Larry dealing with a problem on their own. Larry came down with an upset stomach, and all the nuns could offer him was some Fernet Branca, a digestivo. The nuns could not contact Yvonne because she had gone to Turin, so Susan took to consoling her brother. When Yvonne went to pick them up, she found Larry sitting in his sister's lap and being held. The nuns said they had been like that for some time, and the comforting helped relieve Larry's distress. Yvonne told her daughter how proud she was of how she helped her brother. Susan's response was, "It felt good, Mommy." When Ines heard the story, she told all her friends.

On Sundays, Ines's brother, Baldo, would often ride his bike to have dinner with the family. Being a bachelor all his life, this was a new experience for him, and he and the children enjoyed spending time with each other. On some weekends, Ines's cousin, Irma, from Turin would come to visit, and Yvonne would sometimes take everyone for a short car ride in the countryside. Irma would sit in front with Yvonne; Ines sat in back with Susan and Larry, while Ray slipped into a little space behind the backseat. Sometimes Larry would join Ray in his special seat, and then there would be room for Lorenzo.

With current seat-belt regulations, the Volkswagen would not have been a suitable vehicle for the family.

After three months working in Turkey, I was able to get away for a three-week vacation; and of course, I headed for Ivrea. I spent a week getting reacquainted with my family, but then Yvonne also felt she needed a vacation and convinced Ines to take care of the children while we took a short trip in our Volkswagen. Having a good time was something Ines would sometimes frown upon, but I believe having the children all to herself was appealing to her. She took them for walks, shopping at nearby stores, and watched them as they played in the little inflatable pool Yvonne had brought from the States. After preparing their supper, she would tuck them into their beds and finally she rested. Baldo and Irma also came to help Ines entertain the children. It was a period in which she made the strongest connection with her grandchildren; however, she was relieved when Yvonne returned.

Living six months in Italy rekindled in Ines thoughts of her childhood and created a desire to soon return.

Connecting with Piedmont Again

In 1964, eighteen months after Ines returned from living with Yvonne and her grandchildren, her brother Baldo died. His constant smoking of the strong twisted black Italian cigars led to throat cancer. When the severity of his illness was apparent, Ines made a trip to say good-bye to him. He and Ines spent many years apart, but they developed a warm relationship with each other and on occasion she helped him financially. Yvonne also loved her uncle and was so impressed by the rapport he developed with the children. He was a skilled carpenter who made furniture, and on one of our trips we brought back a table he made. I met him once, and his modest, warm personality impressed me.

Since Ines was the only remaining family member, she and Lorenzo had to decide what to do with the house where her brother lived. Lorenzo pointed out that its condition called for a lot of refurbishing to be done to make it a modern dwelling, and he was hesitant about investing the money. Ines's cousin Irma and Irma's brother, Franco, urged them not to sell the house and volunteered to oversee making the necessary changes. Ines realized that this was their chance to establish a home for returning to a place they had left but could never forget. Lorenzo agreed they were not too many years from retiring, so the investment made sense. Irma and Franco diligently applied themselves to the task and created for them a house that they could be proud of.

The small storage building and outhouse surrounded by a chicken coop in the front yard were removed, and a large tree was planted to give shade to the front of the house. The low concrete wall and wooden door protecting the yard were changed to include a tall forged-iron gate with matching railings atop the low concrete wall to give a stylish appearance to the home. The dirt path from the front gate to the house's entrance was replaced by a wide concrete driveway.

Inside the dwelling, walls were taken down and the dirt floor replaced by tile to create a large living room with a dining area. A small kitchen, which now had running water, was built in one corner of the great room; and in the other corner was a small pantry. Behind the kitchen, a half-bath was created that also accommodated a washing machine. Mother Nature and a line across the balcony on the second floor served as the clothes dryer. A wood-fueled potbellied stove that rested on the floor near the kitchen provided heat for the house. Ines and Lorenzo were not planning to spend the winter months in Vestigne. The wooden stairs to the second floor were replaced with tile, but the elegant balustrade built by Baldo remained. There were two bedrooms on the second floor, and a wall was constructed in one of them to make room for a bathroom. The room contained a half bathtub with a shower, a toilet, and a sink. At that time in the village, two toilets in the house was considered a luxury.

When Ines and Lorenzo returned to see what Ines's cousins had created, they were overwhelmed and so proud of what had become of the family's once very rustic and modest home. For many, many years, the place became a haven for Ines, Lorenzo, and my family.

It was an opportune time to have a place to live in Piedmont since so many of Ines's friends from Astoria were returning to their roots. Luigina and Johnny, who lived across the street, returned to Luigina's family home in a small village about an hour from Vestigne. Maria and Jack rented an apartment in Ivrea, and Natalino and Maria went over each summer to see their families in the neighboring town of Borgomasino. All these emigrants from Piedmont never severed their ties with their homeland, and returning to their places of birth seemed like the natural thing to do.

Beginning in the summer of 1965, Ines and Lorenzo made a yearly journey to spend time living in Vestigne. They were now more sophisticated travelers since they were flying instead of taking a boat. When Natalino and Maria were there, life became more interesting because Natalino would rent a car and take Ines and Lorenzo on short rides to visit people and places throughout the province. Ines would return the favors by often preparing nice meals for them. It was a far cry from Ines's early experiences living in Vestigne. She had somewhat of a celebrity status in the village, where she was referred to as the Americana. She disliked the expression because she felt it showed a lack of acceptance on the part of the villagers, but I found years later it was really a term of respect and endearment.

The village had changed since Ines's youthful years of living there. The cobblestone streets were now paved with tar, and the main street was no longer a thoroughfare. A modern highway that went through the outskirts of the village spared it from big trucks and high-speed traffic. The villagers could now safely ride their bikes and walk to do shopping and make their visits. There were four grocery stores that catered to the populace's daily needs for staples and some fresh products, while a single meat market was sufficient. One day a week a travelling market offered some additional food products and basic clothing for sale, so there was no need to leave the village to sustain oneself.

When Ines and Lorenzo were in Vestigne, they had plenty of time to spend with their friends and relatives in the village. It was a favorite activity of Italians to drop in for a short visit and sip together a glass of Passito or coffee and catch up on the local gossip.

Time was also spent each day shopping for food, but this was no chore since dropping into the local stores was also an opportunity to socialize. You would often see people just standing around in the store talking with the owner or each other. Another way Ines and Lorenzo had to meet people was at the weighing station in front of their house. At certain times during the season, farmers would tow carts into the fields to help with the planting or harvesting, and there was a need to know the weight of material being transported. Lorenzo would often sit out in front of his house and greet all those who stopped. Ines usually said she didn't have time for such doings, and she found the noise they usually made to be distracting. However, I believe she enjoyed the attention it brought to her.

On Fridays they would often take the bus into Ivrea to visit the large weekly market in the center of the town. The grounds were filled with big crowds milling around and vendors shouting about their wares, which made it an exciting and interesting place to visit. It attracted all kinds of hawkers: there were food merchants, clothing dealers, and sellers of household products. I remember one time seeing a woman wheeling around a carriage filled with small dogs; some larger ones were on leashes attached to the carriage, which she was offering for sale.

Ines and Lorenzo's summers in Vestigne were always a welcome change from the crowds, bustle, and anonymity of New York City. In the village they owned a house and everyone knew them; they were somewhat luminaries.

During this time Ines also managed to convince her cousin Irma and later her cousin Franco and his wife to come to the States to see her and Lorenzo. When they were here, we also entertained them in Syracuse and kept up our family ties with Piedmont. It was really a happy time for Ines and Lorenzo. They spent summers basking in the Italian sun, and during the rest of the year shared holidays and other celebrations with their daughter and grandchildren.

In the summer of 1973, Ines and Lorenzo received a surprise reversal of visits with my family when we made a trip to Italy. I had been given a part-time assignment to investigate if Italian aerospace companies had products that we could include in offerings to our American military customers. In carrying out this task, I made several visits to Italy; and during one of them I managed to combine business with a family tour of Italy, France, and England. Of course, part of our plans included a short stopover in Vestigne. When we arrived, we were all impressed by the home that Ines and Lorenzo had fashioned, but it was obvious we would tax the sleeping facilities. They were so glad to see us they gave up their bedroom and slept downstairs on the couch and an easy chair.

It had been ten years since the family had lived in nearby Ivrea. The children were now twelve, fourteen, and sixteen, and we hoped the children would understand in a different way about a part of their past. During our stay we relieved the crowded conditions when I took Yvonne with me for a few days on a business trip. We left the children with Ines and Lorenzo, so they also could be aware of the changes that had occurred since they last cared for them. Our arrival created considerable curiosity and interest in the village, especially among the young people. When we returned from my business trip, the front yard was filled with youths; though language was a problem, they all appeared to be having a good time. Ines had also managed to borrow bicycles for our children, so they were never bored visiting their grandparents. It was an experience that made all of us aware of our unique bond with the village.

When Ines would visit us in Syracuse, she would often keep busy preparing food for us. Some of her favorites were ravioli, gnocchi, and an antipasto recipe that was a very time-consuming dish to make. It consisted of a collection of all kinds of fresh vegetables cut into small cubes and parboiled in vinegar, then combined with olive oil, tuna fish, and tomato sauce and briefly cooked. When she made the dish, there was enough to last us for months; we also put some into small jars to give to our neighbors for Christmas. It was a gift they all looked forward to receiving; it was delicious.

Her ravioli was a favorite of the children. Making it was a big production, and when the children got older they would help her by turning the handle on the pasta press. She wouldn't make just enough for the day's dinner, but a sufficient amount to last until her next visit. Lorenzo's contribution was to count how many she made. I remember once she made 900. She wasn't going to come visit us for a while. Fortunately, we had a large freezer.

Ines wasn't always generous about sharing her recipes. I believe it was because she had no written script, and everything she cooked was based upon her memory or what she did instinctively. She gave demonstrations on cooking gnocchi to a neighbor and our son. Yvonne repeatedly said Ines made the lightest gnocchi she ever tasted.

Spending time in America and Italy gave Ines and Lorenzo a great deal of satisfaction. It created for them the appearance of being both worldly and successful, and in comparison to many in the village, this was true. Those years together were probably the best years of their marriage. They had financial security and a family in the States that cared for them, and were living in a village where they were respected and even admired by some people. These are certainly ingredients for happiness, but I am not sure Ines fully appreciated her good fortune. Her attention would often dwell on negative things that happened to her, and she could never forget for long the setbacks and difficulties that she had encountered.

This auspicious lifestyle continued until 1975, when after arriving in Italy, Lorenzo's health began to rapidly deteriorate. For years he had suffered from emphysema, and he never stopped smoking. He just put up with the coughing and shortness of breath, but that summer his ailments suddenly became much worse and Ines spent most of her time trying to make him comfortable. Although their relationship wasn't always an affectionate and loving one, Ines knew what her duty was as a wife. The care she gave him as his condition worsened made Lorenzo on many occasions offer thanks for her righteous dedication. He finally needed more support than Ines could provide, and he was admitted to the hospital in Ivrea. It was obvious to most people who saw him that Lorenzo was dying, but Ines could not accept the idea. After witnessing his convolutions as he died gasping for air, Ines went into shock.

She called our home in Syracuse, and only my daughter was there to console her while she tearfully informed her of her grandfather's passing away. Susan, who was aware of some of their marital problems, was surprised by the depth of Ines's grief. I guess when something is taken from us, we gain an appreciation for our loss.

On hearing the news, Yvonne got on a flight that allowed her to arrive in Vestigne the next day. The day after, Lorenzo was buried in a family vault in Ivrea. The lack of embalming traditions in Italy makes it necessary to have quick burials.

Yvonne spent three weeks comforting her mother, and during that time Ines showed little appreciation for the effort she made in rushing to give her support. Her attitude was that this is what a daughter was supposed to do. When Yvonne announced she had to return to help our daughter prepare to go to college, Ines commented that she expected to have her stay longer. Being consoled and having the village witness her daughter's devotion was important to Ines. Public demonstrations of deference were always more significant than personal demonstrations of affection. She never looked for an embrace or kiss to bond with a person. In fact, at times she physically discouraged such displays. I remember at her fiftieth anniversary party seeing her push Lorenzo away as he tried to kiss her.

Ines returned to her New York City apartment in the fall, but living by herself and having many of her friends move away made her discontented. The attraction of the city was disappearing, and she spent most of her time that winter visiting my family in Syracuse. It was a precursor of what her future would be.

Turning into the Well-Traveled Woman

In April 1976, the year after Lorenzo died and she was seventy-two, Ines returned to Vestigne. At the same time she was also giving up her rent-controlled apartment in New York City; she made her landlord quite happy. Upon her return, she would come to live with my family in Syracuse. After so many years of living in Astoria, she was ready for a change. Shortly after she left, Yvonne and I and my youngest son, Ray, came down to move her belongings. I rented a very large trailer, and early the next morning the three of us along with a neighborhood friend started moving all her things into the trailer. It was a tiring undertaking, but by early afternoon we had loaded thirty years of Ines's furniture and other possessions she considered precious. After arriving in Syracuse, we waited until the next day to decide where to put everything. Since Ines wasn't returning until the fall, when my daughter would be away at college, most items went in our large basement.

When Ines returned, she slept in our daughter Susan's room, the smallest of our four bedrooms. During the holidays when Susan came home, the boys bunked together. This arrangement continued until Larry went off to college and Susan left home to work in the Washington DC area. At that time we brought Ines's bed and dresser up from the basement and moved her into the largest of our bedrooms. She now felt like she had a place of her own.

Until 1988 Ines would leave Syracuse in the spring and return to us during the fall. Spending winters in Syracuse is not something most people would recommend; but the cold, damp, and foggy climate of Vestigne in the winter, with only a potbellied stove for comfort, is probably less desirable. Besides, I know she enjoyed sharing in the life of my family; and we, in turn, enjoyed her presence. Of course, the respite every year from each other renewed our lifestyle independence and helped restore our appreciation of getting together again.

Our biggest problem when Ines was with us was finding things to keep her busy, but she always managed to make herself useful. Yvonne found many ways for her mother to help in performing household chores. For some of the years Ines lived with us, Yvonne was either attending college or working, so she was appreciative of any assistance she could receive. Ines would help prepare the food or on occasion completely get a meal ready. Ines could knit and mend clothes and was a skilled operator of her sewing machine, and Yvonne knew how to take advantage of her talents. One project Yvonne got her mother involved in was making an elaborate large bedspread. It took a couple years to complete because it required so much complicated and tedious needlework.

Yvonne had found a pattern for the design in one of her craft magazines. It consisted of thirty-eight 16-by-12-inch rectangles of crocheted white yarn, with a green border surrounding arrangements of small different-colored flowers. The rectangles were joined by four-inch-wide strips of the same embroidered white yarn, with a string of colored flowers running over the eight-foot length of the strip. Ines did a lot of the tedious work of forming the white rectangles, while Yvonne embroidered all the colored flowers and borders. When all the pieces were together, it made an impressive spread. It has adorned one of our beds for the last thirty years. Ines would complain while she was doing the work since it took her so long; she was always in a rush to finish something. However, she persisted in her task and was very proud of what she and Yvonne had accomplished.

Ines became so skilled at doing different crafts that she could do them as she watched her soap operas. I remember so often walking in while she was watching couples getting in and out of bed. I teased her about how bawdy the shows were, but she was never embarrassed. In spite of all the things we gave Ines to do, she still found time to read. When she was in Italy, she would buy a weekly gossipy Italian magazine that also contained an attached short romance story that she saved and brought back to the States when she returned. She could read English quite well, but she preferred reading and writing in Italian.

Another thing she liked to read was her Merrill Lynch reports that came every month. In the early 1960s, she started investing in the stock and bond market with the advice of an experienced friend. Over the years she enjoyed seeing the growth of her savings. When she moved to Syracuse, a son of a personal friend became her financial advisor, and once a year he came to the house to review her portfolio. She would complain if her wealth wasn't increasing fast enough, but he always seemed to convince her she was doing well. Her net worth was always a great source of pride for her.

When she felt she needed exercise, she would walk around a long hilly block in the neighborhood and sometimes would help me remove snow from our driveway. When the weather was good, she even took off for a large shopping center about a mile from our house. When she returned with a shopping bag, a neighbor would usually recognize her and drive her home. She had a way of getting people to help her.

When Ines was in Vestigne, she became very close to her next-door neighbor, Giuliana, who was a few years younger than Yvonne and cared for her two elderly parents. She worked in the food market of a large department store and would always stop by on her way to work and ask if there was anything Ines wanted her to bring home. In evenings, she often came over to watch TV with Ines; they became like mother and daughter. The only complaint Ines had about Giuliana was that it was hard to repay her for all her generous favors since she would never accept any gifts. As Ines grew older, she became quite dependent on the help that Giuliana offered.

Another person Ines relied upon was Giovanni, a very generous handyman who was distantly related to her. He would repair problems in the house and winterize the place when Ines returned to the States. He even assisted her when she made major purchases like a TV set; there was little he wouldn't do to make life easier for Ines. She sometimes complained that it took Giovanni a long time to do something; but since he wasn't charging Ines anything for his services, her criticism was hard to understand.

Living in the village surrounded by relatives and friends made life very pleasant for Ines. In her later years, this support became even more important to her quality of life. She could often count on somebody dropping off some vegetables from their garden or some fresh eggs or milk.

Being alone, Ines worried about her security; as a form of protection she would sometimes hang a pair of pants on a clothesline to give the impression that there was a man around the house. There was reason to be concerned, because on two occasions her home was violated. In Italy and other European countries are people called gypsies, who will take advantage of the populace in sneaky and clever ways. In one incident, two women came into her front yard and started up a conversation; after awhile one of them tried to slip off and enter the house. Ines started to yell, and the intruders were scared off.

Another episode, when a man came to the door claiming to be from the utility company, was more serious. He asked to see a receipt, which required Ines to go upstairs. While she was away, he spied her purse and reached in and took her credit card. When she returned, his words and actions made Ines suspicious; she felt threatened by him, but managed to get him to leave without any confrontation. Later, she noticed that her purse had been disturbed, and then become aware her credit card was missing. Ines became very upset and immediately called Giovanni, "Mister Fixit." He gave her good advice: to call her daughter and get her to cancel the card.

At four o'clock in the morning, we received a call from Italy with a very disturbed Ines on the line. Fortunately Yvonne had the same card and knew who to call. She assured her mother that if you call quickly, your liability is limited to $50. Ines began to feel better.

Shortly afterward, we received information that in twenty-four hours and within a short distance from the village, over $5000 had been charged to the card. Ines reported the incident to the police, but after they found out she wasn't hurt, they brushed her off. White-collar crimes are obviously not taken too seriously.

In 1980, Yvonne and I wanted to celebrate our twenty-fifth anniversary by combining a ski vacation with a sightseeing tour. Our plans were to first ski at several resorts in Italy near Vestigne, and then fly to Madrid and travel around Spain and Portugal. We left in March of that year with Ines and helped her get settled into her house. During our stay with her, she showed us off to many of the village people and relatives; as a reward for gracefully accepting this often time-consuming activity, she treated us to a meal at a very nice restaurant. She invited her cousin, Franco, and his wife, and Cousin Irma, but her achievement was to get Guilana to join us. The owner of the place where we were eating was a good friend of Franco's and was determined to give us the royal treatment. During the course of a three-hour meal, we sampled everything the restaurant had on its menu that day. Of course, the samples were quite small, so we never felt physically uncomfortable. Several bottles of wine and after-dinner liqueurs also helped the digestive process. We all had a sense of accomplishment at having survived the owner's generosity.

While in Italy, we went in the afternoon to four different ski areas in Piedmont. After arriving at each, we had a nice dinner and a good night's sleep to prepare ourselves for the next day of skiing. Late in the afternoon, tired from our day on the slopes, we had enough stamina left for the hour–and–a-half ride back to Vestigne, where Ines always had a nice meal waiting for us. It was a pleasant and satisfying way to enjoy a ski holiday, and Ines took pleasure in sharing her home with us.

When it was time to leave for the Iberian Peninsula, we had no use for the skis we had brought with us, so we convinced Ines she could bring them back when she returned in the fall. She always remembered the strange looks she got from airport personnel who wondered what a little old woman was doing transporting two pairs of skis.

In 1984, the year of Ines's eightieth birthday, we persuaded her to celebrate the milestone by going on a TWA getaway tour with us. At the time, I had a full time job to advance our department's advanced technology in Europe, and with the frequent flyer miles I accumulated I was often able to bring Yvonne with me on my trips. We planned to extend one of my visits to tour the southeast coast of Italy and a large part of Sicily. Since Ines's previous traveling was limited primarily to Rome, the itinerary of the tour appealed to her and she made a minor reduction in her net worth and joined us. It was probably the highlight of her travel adventures.

The tour guide was a capable woman who cared for her clients and was extremely good at solving problems that would arise. For example, caught in a traffic jam in Naples, she walked in front of the bus and led it the wrong way down a major street to where it could make a left turn and escape the tie-up. On another occasion, when a small car blocked the path of the bus, she went out on the street and got four men to pick up the car and put it on the sidewalk. She wrote a book describing all the points of interest on the tour and some history associated with each place. She was quite a woman and made our trip very special.

The tour group was not large, only about twenty of us, and all were Italian Americans. Ines was the oldest traveler, and since Italians have great respect for older people, they were quite solicitous in offering her assistance; I think sometimes she felt like a queen. On the night of her eightieth birthday, we were all gathered together at dinner, and several people got up and toasted her continued good health.

An incident occurred that must have made people wonder if Ines needed all the assistance she was being offered. Our tour guide warned us in Palermo that young men might run by and snatch your pocketbook, so be careful to protect it. Ines seriously heeded this advice, but in a way few people would consider. She always liked a drink of sweet vermouth before dinner, and when we arrived in Palermo, she decided to go buy herself a bottle. As she was walking the streets by herself, she approached a group of young men who were behaving in somewhat of a rowdy manner. Ines thought they appeared to be the kind that might snatch a woman's purse. She walked up to them and said, "I am a policewoman and you boys better behave yourselves." As she marched off, I could just imagine the flabbergasted looks on the faces of the youths produced by Ines's aggressive behavior. It was a perfect example of the fact that a good defense is created by a good offense.

The tour was really unforgettable for all of us, but especially for Ines. In all her eighty years, when she was in Italy she seldom ventured far from the environs of Ivrea, but now she had been able to see places she might have just read or heard about.

We started our journey in Rome, and went to Montecasino and Pompeii before boarding a boat that took us to Palermo. After leaving the city, we went west to Trapani and then headed south to Selinute and Agrigento. Although a lot of cultures settled and ruled in Sicily, the Greeks with all their temples seem to have left the most behind to mark their stay. Traveling east to Siracusa, we visited more Greek archeological sites.

Probably the most memorable locale of our trip was our visit to the beautiful town of Taormina perched above the sea and facing Mt. Etna. After returning to mainland Italy, we had a ride along probably the most spectacular road in the world, the Amalfi Drive. It led to a pleasant stop at Sorrento, and then we took a rough boat ride to the idyllic isle of Capri.

After returning to Rome, we rented a car and drove Ines to Vestigne, where we stayed for a few days before flying out of Milan to come home. That summer Ines had a lot to talk about with her friends in the village.

For the next several years I made trips to Europe that sometimes took me to Italy during the non-winter months. At times I brought Yvonne with me; and when I did, Ines expected us to pay her a visit. Between visiting Ines, conducting business, and taking some vacation time, I traveled many of the roads in northern Italy. These frequent visits to Vestigne obviously pleased Ines, and she prepared nice meals for us; her liquor cabinet was always filled with good Italian aperitifs and after-dinner drinks. She generously offered us her hospitality, but somehow was not too generous to herself. I remember on a very warm day driving into Ivrea to do some shopping. Yvonne and I parted company with Ines and planned to meet later on a corner near where we had parked the car. Near the corner was a nice café in the shade, but when we returned we found Ines standing impatiently by the car in the hot sun. When I asked why she wasn't across the street sipping a nice cold drink waiting for us, the look on her face indicated enjoying pleasures like that never occurred to her.

In 1988, all my traveling to support General Electric in the marketing of their advanced technology led to my appointment as the technical director and their senior representative of a European consortium. The position required me to take up residence in Munich, Germany, and so began another phase of Ines's traveling experiences.

We rented and furnished a nice apartment in May, and in July Ines flew from Turin to pay us a visit and see the place. She immediately fell in love with our home and Munich, and we wondered when and if she was going to return to Italy. It was easy to understand her attraction. The apartment bordered on the English Gardens; and when you exited the place, you strolled on sidewalks with tree-lined streets that led to charming shops. In the apartment, Ines had her own bedroom and bathroom and a patio to sit in to enjoy the fresh air. After three weeks, she left; she was happy to hear we would come to Italy in early November to pick her up to spend the winter with us.

We crossed the Alps many times over the next four years to transport Ines or vacation in Italy. I got to know all the passes and tunnels that led to the country. With Ines, however, I usually took her over the Brenner Pass into Austria and then into Germany. When she was with us, she accompanied Yvonne as she went about her job of running our household. Munich is filled with many means of public transportation, and Yvonne became adept at getting around the city and bringing her mother with her. Ines loved to walk around the pedestrian central square of Munich with all its wonderful shops. Stopping for lunch at the department store restaurant that overlooked the Marien Platz and having a bowl of their famous goulash soup would always make her day special.

Shopping in Munich can be a wonderful experience, because the shops have so much to offer and often their sales are real bargains. One day, I was with Yvonne and Ines and witnessed an interesting occurrence. We were in Kaufmart, a large store that seemed to sell everything and at prices that attracted large crowds. I remember seeing people pushing two and three carts, trying to load up on the bargains being offered. Ines was trying to help by going to pick up some turkey cutlets that were on sale. They were such a good price that there were none left in the display case, but somehow she knew they would shortly be out with some more. I then saw the butcher come and hand Ines a package; and at the same time, a German woman came up behind her and tried to pull it from her hands. Ines would not let go and she walked off with her prize, leaving behind a very embarrassed woman. Ines had practice defending her valuables, because on two occasions in New York City she thwarted two attempts to take away her purse. She is one that doesn't give up something without a fight. As she got older, this spirit helped her survive as life was weakening her physically.

Munich was so different from what Ines had experienced in New York and in Italy. Living adjacent to the English Gardens allowed her to take walks through picturesque settings. One view she enjoyed was the island in the Isar River where many Germans sunbathed in the nude. For an Italian who enjoyed her wine, she also adapted to the pleasure of drinking from a stein at the beer gardens in the park.

During one of our years in Munich, Ines accompanied relatives from Ivrea who filled two cars with people to pay us a visit during Oktoberfest. It was a hectic, but pleasing, weekend that allowed Ines to experience this festival that occurs every year in Munich. The city became a place where Ines could feel comfortable, and I know when we finally returned to the States she was somewhat disappointed.

During my years of working in Munich, the company paid for a trip home for Yvonne once a year. I returned during Christmas for two weeks; and Yvonne, with her mother, would leave Munich two weeks before and return two weeks after I returned. During this period the company would help us open our house again so everyone was able to enjoy the comforts of home. Yvonne and I would travel business class; somehow on all her trips across the Atlantic, Yvonne managed to get her mother's coach-class ticket upgraded to business class. Ines was not only a well-traveled woman, but was now doing it in style.

While we were in Munich, my oldest son, Larry, decided to get married and wanted to make it more memorable by having the wedding take place near his grandmother's house in Italy. Yvonne and I were more than happy to assist him by making arrangements for the church and the reception to follow. Of course, most of the burden fell on Yvonne, who had to do all the communicating. I was there to provide the transportation and be a sounding board for the information we collected. During our visit to pick up Ines in the fall, we collected data for Larry and his future bride to consider; and during our return home for Christmas, we discussed it with them. They selected a typical Piedmont restaurant located 2000 feet above the city of Ivrea. They agreed that the small chapel we located in the town was just what they were envisioning. When we returned to drop off Ines in the spring, we made the final arrangements for the wedding. We had to select the reception menu, find a priest, arrange for flowers, have music at the church, and get a photographer to record the whole day. In addition, we needed to set up transportation for the guests to travel up and down the winding roads to the restaurant.

Ines contributed a lot to helping make arrangements; her cousin, Secondo, was a priest and he said he would be honored to perform the ceremony. Her neighbors three houses down the street were a talented family. The son and daughter-in-law were music teachers and volunteered to play during the ceremony. The father was a photographer, who also offered his services. Another cousin in Ivrea owned a company that provided bussing services, so that problem was also taken care of. Larry and his fiancée, Blair, arrived a couple days before the wedding, and Ines showed them where to buy flowers.

Yvonne convinced her mother to host a party in the evening for the wedding guests and to invite people from the village to join in the celebration. A tennis club nearby could serve as the venue for the affair.

The wedding took place on July 16, and it was a typically sunny and warm day. The small chapel housed around thirty Americans, mostly family members, but several of the bride and groom's friends had planned European vacations around attending the event. Some of Ines's friends who were curious about these Americans who came to Italy to get married were also in attendance. In addition to Larry and Blair being joined in matrimony, both parents were renewing their vows. Further involvement by the family included the siblings reading prayers selected by the wedding couple. Even Ines went up to the altar and spoke a prayer in Italian. Except for each couple responding to their vows, the ceremony was completely conducted in Italian. This wasn't really much of a problem since everyone was familiar with the proceedings and Father Secondo used helpful gestures when he wanted participation. For many of us, the beautiful chapel and the unique event taking place within it made the day memorable.

The wedding guests then filed into a small bus for the ride up to the restaurant. It was my third time up the winding mountain road; but this time, since I wasn't driving, I could enjoy the panoramic views that unfolded at almost every turn. After departing from the bus, you could feel the coolness in the air and look down to see the rocky floor of the valley below. It was a Monday, and our party had exclusive use of the restaurant. The owner had arranged a large banquet table adorned with attractive place settings interlaced with bread, grissini, and bottles of wine. The dinner was an extravagant display of Piedmont cuisine and included five typical antipasti followed by gnocchi and risotto. Trout, rabbit, and venison made the entrées a unique and appetizing demonstration of the region's food.

Ines spent most of the time catering to her cousins, Irma and Franco, and his wife Ines, who were the only non-English-speaking people at the party. She seemed so proud that her grandson had decided to come to Ivrea to get married, and she was looking forward to the party she was hosting later.

After changing into more casual clothes, all the reception guests regrouped at the tennis club on the outskirts of Vestigne. Ines had beer, wine, little snacks, and pastries for her guests. She had never given a party this big before and was enjoying being the grand hostess, although she was disappointed by how many people from the village attended the function. The manager of the club was amazed at how much Americans drank and how tall they were. That evening, several of the American guests had to catch a train in Turin and were planning to drive their rented cars to the station. Ines's nephew, Renzo, knew they would have difficulty finding their way at night; so like many helpful Italians I met, he offered to be their guide and lead them to the station. It had been an eventful and gratifying day. It was so satisfying to Ines and my wife and me that our son Larry had achieved his wish of making his wedding such a unique and cherished affair.

In December 1991, Yvonne, Ines, and I returned to live again at our home in Syracuse. We had no children living at home, so we could make accommodations more comfortable for Ines. We bought a single bed that gave Ines more space in her room, but it could open up to a king-size bed if we needed it for company when Ines wasn't with us. In another upstairs room we had a TV that Ines could use to watch the shows she liked. At night she could escape upstairs to be by herself. It gave her a sense of being on her own.

Six months after returning from Germany, I retired from General Electric; and at the same time Ines went back to making her yearly journey to Vestigne. She was now eighty-eight years old, but seemed to have no trouble in making the trip. I was now retired, and like many others I looked forward to doing some traveling. One of the things I convinced Yvonne we wanted to do was live for a while as ski bums. The children of some friends persuaded us the place to carry out our fantasy was where they lived in the Lake Tahoe region of northern California. So, in March 1992, we rented for one month a house on Donner Lake just outside the charming village of Truckee. It is a great place for a skier since the area has several ski areas within a short driving distance and the snow base is measured in feet. In fact, when Yvonne, Ines, and I arrived, snowbanks hid the village from our view. Yvonne and I anticipated great skiing, but Ines wondered what she was going to do. We didn't ski on the weekends and we took some time off during the week to rest, so Ines wasn't alone too much. Her routine was much the same as it was at home: watch the soaps, help prepare the meal, and tag along whenever we went someplace. For exercise, instead of snow shoveling, she tackled the job of trying to remove the hardpacked snow where I parked my car. I managed to convince her that it was a hopeless task.

Her stay was made pleasant by the lovely view of the lake she could enjoy, the visit of her grandson with his wife and their two-year-old daughter, and the scenic drives we took around the picturesque countryside. Her adventures must have made for interesting conversation around Vestigne.

Ines returned with us when we came back the following year. This time we rented a house 1500 feet above the village of Truckee, but somehow her interest had waned and she became bored. When we returned for the third year, Ines decided that spending a month in Florida with her recently widowed friend, Maria Bonafide, was a destination that she preferred. However, she never wavered in her desire to travel each year to Italy. It was her way of showing everyone that, in spite of her age, she was still an able-bodied independent person. I remember once Ines made a slip in her speech when she said, "If I die." I guess when you live a long time, you must get a feeling of being immortal.

Ines' Declining Years

For Ines, returning each year to Vestigne was a sign of her immortality. For her age she enjoyed good health. She took some hypertension medication, but she loved to walk and seemed to suffer little from arthritis pain. She moved slowly up and down the stairs, but I never heard her complain except to doctors who didn't show her the proper courtesy. In her nineties she once went to an examination and asked the doctor what all the dark blotches on her skin were caused by. The doctor said, "Signora, they are a sign of your age." Ines replied, "I didn't come here to be insulted." I always remember her telling me that her body was becoming frail, but her early active years were always kept fresh in her mind so she wasn't going to accept a slur to her well-being.

Over the several years until her death at ninety-eight, she had some mishaps that showed her vulnerability, but also demonstrated her fierce determination to live. The first occurred went she got off the bus in Vestigne after shopping in Ivrea. She had her arms filled with packages and slipped and fell. Her packages were scattered over the street, but the only damage to her body were the bruises on her face and the eventual black eye that developed. Because of her age, the other passengers were concerned. Fortunately, old reliable Giovanni was nearby and after helping her up, drove her home. She ached for a while afterward and her appearance caused a lot of comment from her friends, but she never went to see a doctor. When she returned to us that fall, she made light of the incident.

However, two years later, in 1994, she had a more serious accident. Coming down the stairs in her house and being careless, she fell and this time broke her arm. It was the week before she was going to return to us. At the hospital they put her arm in a cast. After a week to recover from the shock of the incident, she flew to Syracuse. Yvonne took Ines to an orthopedic doctor, who confirmed her arm was healing well, and in eight weeks her cast came off. She then said she was ready to assume some household chores. Ines always wanted to keep busy.

One way she kept busy when she returned from Italy was to go visit our neighbors. Our neighborhood was quite unique, since there were four families who lived next door or across the street with whom for many years we shared together the joys and burdens of raising a family. Ines would drop in like she did in Vestigne and say she was back again. Saying hello was important to Ines, and sometimes she made them feel a little embarrassed that they hadn't come over sooner themselves to greet her. After a few years, our friends caught on and dutifully made their welcome-home visit.

Four years after I retired, Yvonne and I got the urge to visit Europe again. It was a rather ambitious undertaking. We first went to visit friends near London, and then took the Chunnel with them to meet mutual friends near Calais, France. Afterward, we flew to Munich to spend several days revisiting our favorite spots in the city. We then left Germany in a rented car and drove to the Milan airport to pick up my brother and his wife and guide them on a ten-day tour of Italy. After dropping them off at the airport in Rome, we went to Vestigne to pick up Ines, who was going to fly home with us. Ines was now ninety-two, and she appreciated having someone to travel with her this time since her flight had a stopover in London.

The day we came home was quite eventful. We left with plenty of time to spare for the Linate Airport, which is west of the city. About ten miles beyond our entrance to the autostrata, Ines announced she had left her passport at her house. It was another ten miles to where I could exit and turn back. I decided there was not enough time to obey the law, so I made an illegal U-turn and went back to the toll booth I had just entered. I knew Yvonne would have great difficulty explaining our situation, but she gave it a try. I could see we were getting nowhere, so I decided to just take off. I suspect the toll collector didn't know what to do; and by the time he could think of something, I was long gone. I returned to the same entrance a short time later and managed to pass through a different booth without a scene. The rest of the trip was not without incident: we encountered a traffic jam and stopped to have Yvonne ask the police which was the quickest route around the loop road to get to the airport. We arrived with little time to spare, found a wheelchair for Ines, and rushed off, arriving at the gate just as they were boarding. The first thing I did after we took off was to have a glass of wine to calm my nerves. Ines's forgetfulness made for a real exciting ending to our trip, but it was an experience I would gladly have done without.

Yvonne and I often approached Ines with the idea of staying with us year-round, but she would never seriously consider the suggestion. As long as she could walk around the hills in our neighborhood, she felt she could cope with being alone in Vestigne. Actually, she wasn't alone in the village. There were many people who would stop by to see how she was doing, offer to help her, or drop off some food for her. The place was a little like an assisted living facility. So once again, at the age of ninety-three, she returned to her humble abode in Vestigne.

The summer passed uneventfully, and Ines was preparing to return again to Syracuse when another mishap occurred. This time she was going up the stairs carrying too much; when she fell again, she landed at the bottom of the stairs. She banged her head and ribs and was in severe pain. She crawled to a nearby phone and tried calling several people, but no one was home. After lying on the floor for a while, she finally got Giovanni to answer his phone. He came right over and called an ambulance to take Ines to the hospital. The next day, when he knew more about Ines's injuries, Giovanni called us. Ines had several cracked ribs, but the injury to her head was not serious. However, they discovered Ines had developed an ulcer. Giovanni said it would be some time before she could return to the States by herself and we could help with her recovery if we came to Italy. So a day later Yvonne and I were on a plane to see how we could help.

Shortly after we arrived, we went to the hospital and found Ines in a room with seven other women. She was obviously not feeling well and had a pained, sad look on her face. After talking to her, we found out that her ribs were quite painful and that she had been lying in bed ever since they brought her to the hospital several days earlier. Because of her ulcer, the only nourishment she had received during that time was some warm milk a few times a day. Yvonne was shocked at the treatment her mother was being given. She was upset and stormed off to see the doctor. When he saw the fire in Yvonne's eyes, the smile disappeared from his face. To his surprise, she addressed him in fluent Italian. "Doctor, my mother is Ines Ganio, and you have confined her to her bed for almost a week. Since she has always been an active woman, I cannot understand why you are treating her this way."

"Signora, because of her advanced years I assumed she is an invalid."

"You mean, you didn't ask her? My mother is not deaf, and she has always been ambulatory." His answer had made Yvonne even more upset, but she tried to control her frustration and launched into her second concern. "In the United States they found that antibiotics were often more effective in treating an ulcer than a milk diet."

His answer was again a big disappointment. "Yes, I read where they can be effective, but we have also found a milk diet to be effective."

The doctor was not used to dealing with someone like Yvonne because, to Italians, doctors are like gods and their actions are not questioned. However, Yvonne was polite and he was not too offended by being questioned. Besides, her command of the local language made her seem like one of them instead of the American he knew she was. He seemed like a nice person, but not a very competent doctor. Trying to reassure Yvonne, he said, "We will build up her strength so you can take her home."

The hospital responded to Yvonne's dietary complaints the next day by giving Ines a meal a healthy person would have difficulty consuming. Yvonne told the nurse that she would like to take her mother home before they killed her. The nurse gave Yvonne an understanding look, showing she had some sympathy with her assessment. Ines was not a good patient; she couldn't sleep at night and demanded attention from the skeleton staff. The nurses suggested we hire someone to spend the night with her. In Italy, this is a common practice when extra assistance is needed; the hospital maintains a list of aides for you to contact. We hired someone for two nights to keep Ines company and take care of her. Finally Ines got permission to leave the hospital, and with Yvonne and me for support, she managed to get home. We looked into getting a special bed that would allow her to sleep on the first floor, but Ines wanted no part of this idea. She felt she would be comfortable enough resting and sleeping on a couch in the living room.

Our efforts to rebuild her strength were having some positive effect, but she still complained about the soreness from her bruised ribs. We made the mistake of asking a doctor who periodically visited the village for some medication to ease the pain. We didn't realize it, but he gave her an aspirin-type drug. This relieved her aches, but the next day she had blood in her bowels and we knew her ulcer must be bleeding again. Her weakened condition told us we had to get help for her, so we returned this poor woman to the hospital. The drug she had been given amazed the hospital doctor, and he changed her treatment by giving her some medication for her ulcers, a couple of transfusions, and some bland food to eat. I felt very sorry for Ines, and her poor condition made us become concerned about how long it would be before we could bring her back to the States. To our surprise, Ines—who was ninety-three at the time—in the span of three days made a miraculous recovery and we took her home. We arrived back in the States in time to spend Thanksgiving with my son Larry and his family before returning the next day to Syracuse.

Ines had survived another of her mishaps; and after six months of a low-salt diet, walks around the block, and Yvonne's substantial care, she was ready to again return to Italy. She continued to travel back and forth like she had done for the last many years. During the Thanksgiving and Christmas holidays, she went wherever we went to be with our family. Yvonne knew how to give her Christmas gifts she really seemed to appreciate. Jewelry and nice clothes always appeared to make her happy. Over the years she accumulated a nice wardrobe of fine clothes. On Sunday evenings, when Ines went to the senior citizen functions in the village, everyone was always impressed by how well she was attired. For the cold winters in Syracuse, she bought herself a beautiful mink coat, which she wore to church on Sundays.

Ines had trouble being impressed with gifts that were mainly thoughtful. One Christmas, my son Larry's family gave her a cooking apron with large pictures of his three daughters imprinted on it. It was attractive and not inexpensive, but Ines was not impressed with its value and let it be known. She was not one to be silent about her feelings, and her comments dampened somewhat the Christmas spirit. However, she contributed to the holiday atmosphere by making ravioli or her sausage stuffing, which were everyone's favorites. Another tradition was the making of sweet fried dough to nibble on for a snack.

Each year we wondered if Ines would want to return to Italy, but she never hesitated to prepare herself. Finally, in 2001, at the age of ninety-seven, she made what turned out to be her final trip to Vestigne . A few weeks before returning to Syracuse, another mishap occurred. She had again fallen down the stairs and smashed her face, but miraculously nothing was broken. It was the fourth time in eight years poor Ines had fallen. She often tried to carry too much up and down the stairs; she did little to compensate for her advancing years. Her cane hung from her wrist when she walked, instead of being held firmly in one hand.

However, her biggest problem was not eating properly, which resulted in the buildup of water in her body that, in turn, affected her breathing. So after she fell, she was in dire need of help. Her friends in Vestigne generously responded by preparing food for her, keeping her company, and making sure all her wants were taken care of. We considered going over to bring her back again, but because of the 9/11 mayhem and all the travel difficulties, we were advised against doing it. In late September, the turmoil was beginning to subside; and Ines managed to recover enough to be put on a nonstop flight to Newark, where we were waiting for her. Seeing her weakened condition when she arrived, we weren't sure she could survive the car trip to Syracuse. When we returned home, we had to carry Ines up to her room.

We were glad to have Ines home, but we knew we would have a difficult future. Yvonne put her on a strict salt-free diet, and Ines asserted her strong will to live and was soon able to get around by herself. In fact, after a few months, she was again slowly walking around the block. To Ines, this was a sign that she could again return to Italy. We told her that it was no longer safe for her to return and take care of herself. She resisted our assessment, but she was weakening. Yvonne had been taking complete care of her, and Ines finally agreed that she could not live alone. Her doctor agreed with our concerns, and that reinforced for Ines our judgment. She was beginning to bemoan her fate and feel sorry for herself, and one day she was complaining and dwelling on the unhappy episodes during her marriage. I reminded her she was overlooking the more than thirty years she lived enjoying her independence and her family.

We finally got her to accept going into an assisted living home when we had to take a trip. On several occasions, she tried to make Yvonne promise not to put her in a nursing home. But in May 2002, we felt caring for her was becoming too difficult, and she finally agreed to go into a nice assisted living facility on a permanent basis. We had convinced her it was not a nursing home. We had to lie to her about how much it cost to live in the facility because we feared she would refuse to move in if she knew the truth.

In June we brought her home to celebrate her ninety-eighth birthday with all our neighbors. She was queen for the day, exchanging snappy remarks, eating her favorite dessert, apple pie, and getting a bit woozy on champagne. Everyone was impressed by her performance, but after that she began to slip away. On July 24 she suffered a brain hemorrhage, and doctors said she wouldn't last the night. Two days later, she was giving them orders again. Her spirit just seemed to be unshakable. However, it was her last grasp at living; the great difficulty she had breathing made her long for death, and she passed away on July 30. This almost indestructible woman, who once said to me, "If I die," had to finally accept a fate we all share.

Her funeral was well attended by our many friends, who also knew Ines quite well. Our three children, who admired her strength, were there to make things easier for Yvonne and me. Even our pastor, Father John, was aware of her feisty spirit, and commented during his eulogy that she was probably now giving orders to St. Peter on how to improve paradise. We knew how much she wanted to get back to Italy; as a result, we had her cremated so we could take her ashes to Piedmont and unite her again with her husband, who was buried in Ivrea. It was heartwarming to read all the cards our friends sent to us. So many people told us about little incidents they remembered about Ines that made her unforgettable and unique. I guess always speaking the truth, even when people may not want to hear it, makes a lasting impression.

Over the years Ines spent with us, she often asked Yvonne what she was going to do with her money when she died. Yvonne knew how much Ines abhorred extravagance, so she always gave her the same answer: "We are going to buy a Ferrari and put your ashes in the backseat and take you wherever we go." Ines was never sure if Yvonne was serious or not. I thought it would be in keeping with Yvonne's answer and appropriate if I rented a Ferrari to take her ashes to Vestigne; however, it was not possible to rent one, so I settled for renting an Alfa Romeo.

Prior to Ines passing away, we had initiated efforts to sell her house; so we were going to Italy not only to put Ines's ashes in their final resting place, but to also complete the sale and vacate the house. Ines's good friend and neighbor, Clelia, had made a fair offer and we anticipated no problems.

After making arrangements with the town of Ivrea to open the vault, Yvonne called several relatives and friends to let them know about the plans for interring Ines's ashes. At 10:00 a.m. on the scheduled day, there were sixteen people gathered to say good-bye to Ines. I realized all of them were not only in attendance to comfort Yvonne or me, but because they wanted to pay their last respects to Ines, a woman they all esteemed. We knew everyone, but I hadn't realized that Ines's and Lorenzo's sides of the family didn't know each other. Yvonne performed the introductions, and then we all paraded together back into the cemetery, where the workmen had broken into Lorenzo's burial vault. They had used a ladder to remove the marble protecting the vault, and it rested just below the opening. Yvonne thanked everyone for coming, and the priest said a few short prayers. I held the urn for everyone to touch, and I gave it to a workman who climbed the ladder to place it in the vault.

After giving up the urn, I realized Ines no longer had to worry about returning to Piedmont; she was now here for eternity. As they were closing up the vault, I thought that husband and wife were being united again after thirty years. I reflected about the arguments they often had, and I wondered if it was a good idea. I realized that God must have thought it was the right thing to do because he guided Yvonne, who knew them both so well, to bring about the reunion. It was obvious that day a large burden had been lifted from Yvonne's shoulders. For over a year she had been dealing with the stress of her mother's illness and the pain of her death. For all but the last year of her life, Ines did pretty much as she wanted; but as she lost control of her destiny, Yvonne had to be not only a caregiver, but also a person who had to endure the frustrations expressed when a strong spirit becomes weak.

The last tribute to Ines was the following Sunday when Clelia had a mass said for her. Many people from Vestigne came, but the church became even more crowded by persons from the neighboring town of Borgomasino, along with people from Ivrea. On the Sunday of Ines's mass, a little write-up announcing her death appeared in the church bulletin. The son of a friend wrote it, and his description of Ines was very perceptive and touching. He called her "a woman of strong character, volatile and independent; she had known how to confront the difficulties of the emigrant and, like the swallow who always returns to her nest, until the end, she always returned to her beloved country. The Americana, as she was called, leaves a void." This man really knew and understood Ines. It seems that being considered an Americana was not the negative expression Ines thought, but a word that set her affectionately apart from others in the village.